Adam,

MW01089057

Hope you enjoy the book, and we're likely due for another bar meetup!

Cheers,

Advance Praise

"Brilliant, innovative, creative, intriguing, and
faintly disturbing. The product of a first-rate mind."

—RICHARD KOCH, author of the bestselling *The 80/20 Principle*

———

"A roadmap for ambitious entrepreneurs aspiring for business success."

—PAUL ORFALEA, founder of Kinko's

———

"Whether you're starting, scaling, or selling, this is a must-read. JCron has
been there, done that, and is always on my speed dial when I'm stuck on
strategy or growth. My favorite is the Recognition Referral Revenue Loop."

—NEIL PATEL, *New York Times* bestselling author and creator of
1 of the 100 most brilliant companies by *Entrepreneur* magazine

———

"Whether you're a seasoned entrepreneur or just starting out,
Billion Dollar Bullseye equips you with the tools, mindset, and roadmap
needed to navigate the complexities of business with confidence and clarity."

—FAISAL HOQUE, entrepreneur and #1 *WSJ* and *USA Today* bestselling
author of *Reinvent, Lift,* and *Everything Connects*

———

"JCron is the greatest business mind I know. Talking with him about
business is a psychoactive experience. His ability to see the right path with
pristine clarity and communicate flawlessly constantly blows my mind. So
far, he has a 100% hit ratio with every piece of advice he's given me. In fact,
it's gotten to the point that I'm nervous speaking with him because I KNOW
that whatever he suggests is almost guaranteed to be the right move and
thus the one I have to make. If you're lucky enough to have JCron as a friend
or mentor, it'll be a lethal competitive edge you simply can't replicate."

—RIAN DORIS, cofounder and CEO of Flow Research Collective

"JCron has provided us with invaluable insight—we've used his guidance to grow rapidly and evolve our business in ways that wouldn't have otherwise been possible."

—STEVEN KOTLER, 4x *NYT* bestselling author and cofounder of Flow Research Collective

Billion Dollar Bullseye

Billion Dollar Bullseye

*Scale As Big As You Want, As Fast As You Want,
and Exit (If You Want) On Your Terms*

Jonathan "JCRON" Cronstedt

THINK
TWICE
B O O K S

WASHINGTON, DC

THINK TWICE
B O O K S

Think Twice Books | www.thinktwicebooks.com

All trademarks are the property of their respective companies.

Cover Design: Pete Garceau

Interior Design: Zoe Norvell, INeedABookInterior.com

Cataloging-in-Publication Data is on file with the Library of Congress.

ISBN: 978-1-64687-174-2

Special Sales

Think Twice books are available at a special discount for bulk purchases for sales promotions and premiums, or for use in corporate training programs. Special editions, including personalized covers, a custom foreword, corporate imprints, and bonus content, are also available.

1 2 3 4 5 6 7 8 9 10

For my wife, Nicole, and my daughter, Morgan.
You are the foundation of meaning and purpose
in my life and the greatest source of joy and
motivation imaginable.

For my dear friend and business partner, Kenny Rueter.
Without your sprinkler toy, founder's grit,
determination, and vision for the #KajabiHero,
this would never have been my journey.

For my parents, thank you for always supporting my
ambition and drive.

For all the entrepreneurs, mentors, bosses, and friends
who have shared knowledge and time with me and
influenced my career, thank you.

For the entrepreneurial visionary and founder who
is reading and seeking actionable knowledge to apply to
your own growth story, this book is literally for you.

Jim Rohn always said that poor people have big
televisions and rich people have big libraries, so this
is my attempt to support you with the latter.

CONTENTS

Foreword from Kenny

It all started with a text.

In December 2011, a year after launching Kajabi, a mutual friend sent an email to Jonathan and me, introducing us and suggesting that we might be interested in doing business together. She closed the email with, "Here's to a new partnership!" And wow, was she ever right about that.

I followed up her email with a quick text to Jonathan, which marked the beginning of a lifelong friendship and a life-changing ride on the rocket ship called Kajabi.

And a damn good time we indeed had. Every bit of it.

At that time, Kajabi had just crossed the $1M ARR (Annual Recurring Revenue) mark. Despite this milestone, I was far from comfortable. Our product was rough around the edges, barely meeting my own expectations. To make matters more complicated, we had a vocal customer base eager to point out

every flaw. Every morning I woke up with a gnawing fear: What if today is the day they've had enough of the bugs and decide to quit? I didn't have a roadmap to success or any prior experience building a software company. What I did have, however, was a strong sense of purpose, incoming profits, and a product people actually wanted—key ingredients for success, as you'll read in this book.

JCron and I quickly hit it off, and I was impressed by his expertise in direct response marketing and networking. I brought him on board as a consultant, acting as our affiliate manager to build relationships that could drive new business. This was going great until I took him to Starbucks and fired him because I had the opportunity to retain the services of an even *more* experienced marketer and couldn't afford them both.

Don't feel too sorry for him, though, because JCron returned the favor to me several months later after we re-hired him in a full-time capacity (this time as director of marketing), and he subsequently took *me* to Starbucks and quit so he could take on a CEO role at a company located in Austin. We stayed friends and kept in touch over the years, especially as he found success growing other businesses. At one point, JCron was working for a company based in Dallas, but he rented an office from Kajabi to use when he was in Southern California, so he always had a pulse on our business.

The third time was the charm. In 2016, JCron came back to Kajabi, this time stepping in as president and equity partner. JCron brought what I lacked to the partnership. Coming from a software background, I was technical and analytical by nature. My focus gravitated toward the product and what it needed to do to help our customers the most. JCron, on the other hand, brought a wealth of marketing and sales experience, a deep knowledge of the customers we were serving, and the uncanny ability to instantly conjure up the right words to say in any situation. I nicknamed him the "human teleprompter." His party trick? Spontaneously delivering a pitch-perfect sales script for any of our customers' businesses, no prep needed. The combination of our natural abilities and strengths, coupled with our intense desire to win and our unwavering grit to make that happen, helped us navigate that exciting journey from $6M to over $100M in ARR—in just five years.

Man, I wish I'd had this book back in Kajabi's early days! We didn't have a playbook, so we had to figure it out ourselves as we went along. Our journey was driven by intuition, lots of trial and error, and above all else, ALWAYS solving for the customer first (our purpose). We had a unique advantage at Kajabi: In addition to working every day at growing our own business, we had a front-row seat to our customers' businesses as well. We observed the hurdles our customers faced and learned firsthand what led some ventures to flourish and others to flop. JCron excelled at empathetic listening, pinpointing customer pain points, and guiding them toward effective solutions. What he said always resonated with the customers, and he was able to masterfully analyze their businesses.

I'm thrilled JCron wrote this book. His wealth of knowledge and real-world chops can help countless businesses. Keeping that to himself would've been a real waste. Whether you're just starting out in business, or are already well into your business's growth, this book is a must-read. It is the roadmap that I never had, and when I look in the rearview mirror, I realize that *Billion Dollar Bullseye* perfectly encapsulates the success we attained at Kajabi. This isn't one of those books filled with catchy yet useless advice. It's a hands-on guide to building a standout company. Building a business isn't easy. This isn't a paint-by-numbers book that you read and then expect to have instant success. I know what it's like in the trenches, though, and sometimes when you're too close to the problem, you develop tunnel vision. You either put too much focus on only a single aspect of your business or you overlook fixing the core of your business, and instead, grasp for new marketing tactics to try to stimulate growth.

Consider this book your roadmap. It'll guide you through the seven key components of an epic company, in the order you should tackle them. For each component, you'll get a self-assessment to honestly evaluate your progress, along with a heads-up about common traps others fall into.

Let me be clear: This book isn't just a collection of good ideas—it's a distillation of hard-won lessons from years of triumphs and setbacks. It's as close as you'll get to sitting down over drinks with JCron, a seasoned expert who's seen it all and has the scars and accolades to prove it. We didn't have a roadmap for Kajabi, but you don't have to go in blind. This book is that roadmap, refined through real-world trial and error. Don't just skim through it—dive in. Engage with the self-assessments, question your preconceptions, and prepare for a transformative experience. Give each word the attention it deserves, and you won't just be reading about success; you'll be living it. Here's to building your own epic company and achieving unimaginable success. Turn the page and let your journey begin.

To your success ...

—KENNY RUETER
Kajabi Co-Founder & Executive Director

What Is Kajabi?

Founded in 2010 by Kenny Rueter, Travis Rosser, and Andy Jenkins, Kajabi set out to simplify the creation and marketing of online courses and digital products. Starting as a small startup, it quickly gained traction as the demand for online education and digital content exploded. Kajabi's user-friendly platform, robust features, and commitment to providing a comprehensive solution for online entrepreneurs and educators set it apart from the competition. As online learning and digital product creation continued to surge in popularity, Kajabi expanded its offerings and refined its platform, attracting a diverse user base of entrepreneurs, coaches, authors, and content creators.

In 2023, Kajabi made headlines by announcing that its 60,000 creators had collectively earned a remarkable $5 billion in lifetime gross merchandising value (GMV). This substantial achievement represents a staggering 528% increase in GMV since 2019 and more than doubling since the end of 2021. Notably, this $5 billion figure marks a significant jump from March 2020, when Kajabi reported over $1 billion in creator revenue. Furthermore, Kajabi is now valued at over $2 billion, following a capital raise led by Tiger Global, and including TPG, Owlrock, Meritech, Tidemark, and Spectrum Equity. Kajabi's impressive growth underscores its pivotal role in the online education and digital content creation space, offering a comprehensive suite of tools and resources for launching and growing online businesses while empowering content creators to achieve remarkable financial success.

Introduction

This book exists for two reasons:

1. To connect with the right people and businesses I can advise, partner with, or invest in to broaden our collective global impact.
2. To help you win as quickly as possible so that you're excited about the potential of #1.

You're busy, so I'll get to the point: Zig Ziglar said, "You can have everything you want in life if you will just help enough other people get what they want."[1]

Simply put, **I want to help you get what you want.**

I can't promise this book will magically build you a billion-dollar valuation. What I *can* promise you is that within these pages is a method of scaling that has an undeniable, proven track record. I call this method the Bullseye Formula.

Take, for example, my most recent company, Kajabi. Discovering and implementing the Bullseye Formula, we took our annual revenue from $6M to over $100M and a valuation of over $2B (2,153% growth, all within five years).

Before the thinking that gave way to the Bullseye Formula, every time someone asked me how we got a $2B valuation I'd tell them, "I don't know. It's not like I have a seven-point, almost-never-fail, double-unicorn strategy."

Now I do. And it's in this book.

---

[1] Meier, J. D. "Great Zig Ziglar Quotes." *Sources of Insight*, 2024. https://sourcesofinsight.com/zig-ziglar-quotes/.

You may be wondering, "Is this book really for me? How is this book different from the thousands of others like it? Who is this 'JCron' guy anyway, and why should I trust him?"

All good questions we'll get to, but first, let's talk about you.

This book is for anyone who wants to grow their business to its maximum potential. This book is about taking your idea—the problem you solve for your customers—and scaling it far beyond your personal lifestyle goals.

If you're like most of the entrepreneurs I talk to, you're tired of the intellectual junk food—the tip, trick, and hack approaches that work great for shareables on social media but never bring actual results.

You may be ready to start your business. You may have already begun and are looking to scale. You may even be thriving in the marketplace but still want to reach that next rung on the ladder. Even after Kajabi's $2B valuation, we wanted to expand, to explode, and to reach exponentially higher levels.

Regardless of where you are in scaling, this book will be impactful for you. You will gain clarity on what to focus on, awareness of what needs to be modified, and strategic wisdom for how to position your business for growth and, if you want, exit.

Is this a start-up book selling dreams of three-hour workdays and a luxurious lifestyle that is attainable with little effort? No.

This book is for serious entrepreneurs who understand that **you cannot escape the responsibility of tomorrow by evading it today.**[2] (I didn't make that up—Abraham Lincoln did, a man who knew a thing or two about leadership.)

I wish I could tell you I was born knowing these game-changing principles, but I've had quite the journey to get here.

---

2   BrainyQuote. "Abraham Lincoln Quotes." *BrainyMedia Inc.*, 2024. https://www.brainyquote.com/quotes/abraham_lincoln_101733.

From telemarketing in high school to harassing the owner of a Lamborghini Diablo VT Roadster for coaching advice, I did whatever I could to learn as much as possible about sales, business, and what it takes to be successful.

And it's not been without its pitfalls. I've made it big and lost it all. I once bought my parents a house and had to turn around and help them move out. I lost everything—their house included—in the real estate market back in 2008. If you've been bankrupt, or are bankrupt, take heart; I too earned that T-shirt.

(Here's me, two years before bankruptcy, in a very different T-shirt, with a Lego guy for some odd reason.)

The man at the closing table that day was not the man who returned to the closing table when I had to give back the keys. Not only had I let myself down, but I'd let down two people who had worked incredibly hard to give me the opportunities I felt I'd fumbled. I was ashamed of what I perceived to be a massive professional and personal failure.

As with most defeats, there were lessons to be learned in the aftermath. I took this wisdom and applied it to new ventures. I'm deeply grateful for the success I've found. But believe it or not, I'm just as grateful for the success I've helped other entrepreneurs find. Entrepreneurs like you.

The good news is that you can bypass all the tough lessons I learned from categorical failure and execute with confidence, having the formula that will result in a 7, 8, 9, or 10-figure outcome.

Full disclosure, you should know that 3 out of every 5 million companies have the chance of becoming a unicorn. That's a .00006% chance you have of starting a business and hitting it *that* big.[3]

If that's your goal, congratulations. We're going to talk about the exact formula to shift the odds in your favor of becoming one of the .00006%.

And good on you for setting big goals. Small goals, in my experience, simply have no magic.

Regardless of your financial goal, if you shoot high and implement these strategies, you'll still have a better business than you do right now.

I can guarantee it.

My only disclaimer about this formula is that it absolutely *can* make you rich—rich enough to have an existential crisis.

I recently saw an article from *Harvard Business Review* titled, "Dealing with the Emotional Fallout of Selling Your Business."[4]

Not exactly what you'd expect on the other side of this journey. But when I found myself a board member of Kajabi and no longer its president, that's exactly what I experienced—a season of purposelessness. But even there, in the emotional cellar of "What's next?," I found meaning and learning.

Now, let me be clear. No one is going to feel bad for you after success. But

---

3   The Review. "There's a .00006% Chance of Building a Billion Dollar Company: How This Man Did It." *First Round Review*, n.d. https://review.firstround.com/theres-a-00006-chance-of-building-a-billion-dollar-company-how-this-man-did-it/.

4   Giesea, Jeff. "Dealing with the Emotional Fallout of Selling Your Business. *Harvard Business Review*, September 1, 2015. https://hbr.org/2015/09/dealing-with-the-emotional-fallout-of-selling-your-business.

despite that fact, I'm positive you'll still want to experience that existential crisis for yourself. I'm thankful I did.

If you're like me, you probably got into business because you want to get out of business—whether that means you want to exit or systemize and start collecting passive income checks.

I love growing companies, and if there were a dysfunction to describe my love of entrepreneurship and working with entrepreneurs, I'd self-identify as such.

In an increasingly complex and overly politicized climate, I believe entrepreneurship is the single greatest transformational force in our world and that it may be just the thing that saves it.

Let's roll ...

—JONATHAN "JCRON" CRONSTEDT

Chapter 1

The Bullseye Formula: How It Works

Expanding Your Bullseye

This is the last book you'll ever need to scale your business. It's industry agnostic, meaning it can help you regardless of the market you serve.

These foundational scaling principles are best captured and communicated with the visual of a dartboard.

If you're looking at a traditional dartboard, you may think you'd win by hitting the same bullseye multiple times, but you'd be wrong. There are four spots on a dartboard that are worth more than the bullseye. In our case, the dartboard is a metaphor for your business, and the goal isn't just to hit the bullseye but to expand it.

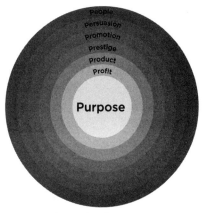

Let me explain.

Figure 1 The Bullseye: Purpose

If you follow the Bullseye Formula correctly, you'll see that moving from the center bullseye outward, then mastering each successive ring, will only increase the size of the bullseye, and in doing so, increase your odds of success.

That's the magic of the Bullseye Formula. You simply can't miss if you're throwing at a bullseye that's bigger than everyone else's.

Each ring of the dartboard is dependent on the one that precedes it, and *so it is with the effectiveness of your business.* Your success in scaling is dependent on giving each ring the proper attention and weight according to the structure of the dartboard.

The three inner rings, Purpose, Profit, and Product, are your core three. They are foundational. They are worth more than any of the outer rings that follow. If you master Purpose, your next area of focus is Profit. Once you've become profitable, your bullseye is not just the size of Purpose but the size of Purpose and Profit. Add in nailing Product, and you've tripled the size of the bullseye and tripled your odds of success.

Figure 2 The Expanded Bullseye: Purpose and Profit   Figure 3 The Expanded Bullseye: Purpose, Profit, and Product

The remaining rings—Prestige, Promotion, Persuasion, and People—are amplifiers. Imagine they're like the spots on a traditional dartboard that double or triple the score. When you have your three core rings interlocked, and you hit the Prestige, Promotion, Persuasion, or People ring—ding! ding!—that hit increases the size of your bullseye exponentially.

Remember, the amplifiers only work if you have the core three nailed down.

If you get stuck or don't solve a product problem and happily skip ahead to the next ring, you will become dependent on other aspects of your business with less and less leverage to grow your venture.

It is essential to follow the formula from the center target outward. Be purpose-driven before you look at profit potential, before you dial in your product, and so on. A lack in one area puts more pressure on the subsequent ring, making it more difficult to build something that can sustain the revenue and growth you need to achieve your Billion Dollar Bullseye.

Believe me, you don't want to miss a ring and find that you're solely reliant on People as your Hail Mary for a successful business. You'll find out quickly that "A-players" don't want to fix a dumpster fire.

Without following the flow of these concentric rings, in order to scale, you'll have to rely on overemphasizing, over-resourcing, or overcommitting to other areas to act as a surrogate or support to compensate for the foundational structure of your business. There's absolutely no blame in that, either. It's not like there was an industry-agnostic formula for how to lay the foundation of your business for scaling to a double-unicorn valuation ...

Until now.

Let's go back to your dartboard. As you're aiming at a larger bullseye, you're going to have more control over outcomes. Which is great—*if you understand that not all rings are created equal.* Some of the rings represent targets that are massive needle movers while some amplify attention or audience, and others are only effective if you've mastered the rings preceding them.

The question is: How do you figure out which ring (target) is important? **Unbalanced performance often isn't realized until you're reaping what you sowed.** The Bullseye Formula is designed to keep you knowledgeable of what rings are important and provide confidence in your approach to mastering each one.

When I look back on my early experience growing a business, I placed way too much of a burden on People, Persuasion, and Promotion to support and supplement the real work I needed to do. If you've ever done the same, you're in good company.

I promise you that the moment you realize how often you've relied on the outer amplifiers within your target, it will shock you. **Let it also inform you.** Entrepreneurs have a passion for the projects they find enjoyable, yet they frequently overlook the critical areas that truly contribute the most potential value to their businesses.

To attain growth in your business, you must reconsider your approach and shift your focus.

And that's where the Bullseye Formula comes in. Focus relentlessly on the seven areas of the Bullseye Formula *in the correct order*, and we'll be toasting your successful exit in the near future.

The Order of Operations

Do you ever wonder why the order of operations isn't clearer in the business advice you come across? Because leaders either don't know or they don't want to do the work. It's easier to sell what the world wants to buy.

The "work" they want to do is to say, "Sales, it's *your* problem. Get better. Marketing, it's *your* problem. Get better."

For example, if you look at many CEO coaches, the "magic" of their framework is simply, "What is your plan?" They dog you about when you'll get it done and threaten to leave you in the dust if you don't do it. That's it. The bluntest of blunt objects.

Or worse yet, a productivity solution or communication methodology that simply makes you more efficient at the wrong tasks, not more effective.

What's missing is an *order of operations*. If you miss this process laid out in target form in this book, then you miss the opportunity to expand your bullseye and scale your business. Hitting these opportunities exponentially increases your likelihood of success.

Think about it this way:

2^7

Also written as:

2 x 2 x 2 x 2 x 2 x 2 x 2

Either way you slice it, you get 128 as the answer.

But what happens when you miss one of those doublings?

2 x 2 x [miss] x 2 x 2 x 2 x 2

No matter how good those other doublings are, you're not going to get your maximum of 128. You will only be partially as successful as you could have been because you missed that one area. Mathematically speaking, you're at 64 (half as successful as 128), and all it took was missing one ring.

If you're looking for an exponential trajectory in your business, you cannot afford to miss any ring in the Bullseye Formula.

This is not an easy game.

Don't Play Small with the Bullseye Formula

Before we dive into the meat of this book, let's agree that **there is no point in playing small.** I'm not suggesting that everyone can receive a double-unicorn valuation, but no matter your business model, you can choose to set the bar high or set the bar higher—whatever that looks like for you.

If you play small, not only will investors lack interest, but you'll be easily beaten by the competition.

People with more money will win. They can buy more ads. They can hire more people. They can take more of your customers and serve them at a higher level. Your repeat business will suffer as you're outpaced by your larger competition time and time again.

Most importantly, your business is a wealth asset. If you're not growing it, you're derelict in your duty.

I'm about to share the statistics and data that demonstrate how playing small goes against every goal you're trying to achieve with your business and how implementing the Bullseye Formula guarantees your ability to scale bigger than you imagined possible.

For now, read this book open to the idea that you are not going to play small. No matter the reasons or resistance you might feel to that idea.

Why?

Maybe you've heard this story before:

Person has a great idea and starts a business. The business grows quickly to several million dollars in sales. Person sells the business for an enormous profit. Person enjoys a life of fancy houses, exotic cars, and more money than they ever dreamed of.

This story is what many entrepreneurs envision when they start out. The problem? This story is a lie.

The stark reality is quite the opposite of the "entrepreneurial urban legend" referenced above.

Can building a business make you rich?

Absolutely.

Don't just take it from me. The top 20 Americans on the Forbes 400 list of wealthiest people gained their wealth through business ownership.[1] That's as true now as it was fifty years ago—and every year in between.

Expand your view worldwide, and there's even more evidence that businesses build wealth. One of the wealthiest people in the world, Bernard Arnault, built wealth as the chairman of a French luxury goods company. He is the founder, chairman, and CEO of Louis Vuitton Moët Hennessy, the world's largest company of its kind. He's created an empire that his kids will inherit and continue to grow.

Owning a business *can* make you rich …

But many businesses fall short. Too many anticipate the easy route— building for a year and "making it big" the next. Entrepreneurs fail to understand exactly what they are building and how to leverage a business as a wealth asset. Staggeringly, **only 2.7% of businesses in the United States do over $1 million in sales annually.**[2]

According to the most recent data from the U.S. Bureau of Labor Statistics, the median annual income for self-employed individuals in the United States was around $51,350 in 2020.[3]

What's going on? How can *Forbes* compile a list of wealthy entrepreneurs while the majority of business owners are drowning in a pool they built for themselves?

I've too often heard the answer, "Luck." People were born into certain

---

1   LaFranco, Rob, and Chase Peterson-Withorn. "The Forbes 400." *Forbes*, 2023. https://www. forbes.com/forbes-400/.

2   United States Census Bureau. "Statistics of U.S. Businesses." *United States Census Bureau*, November 17, 2023. https://www.census.gov/programs-surveys/susb.html.

3   U.S. Bureau of Labor Statistics. "Labor Force Statistics from the Current Population Survey." *U.S. Bureau of Labor Statistics*, May 28, 2024. https://www.bls.gov/cps/earnings.htm.

positions, families, and communities that lifted them higher than any *normal* person could go.

That's straight-up BS.

Warren Buffett has a business partner by the name of Charlie Munger, who said, "To get what you want, you have to deserve what you want. The world is not yet a crazy enough place to reward a whole bunch of undeserving people."[4]

Basing results off "luck" is absolute nonsense.

The method I use, the one you're reading about in this book, has nothing to do with luck, and it won't be nearly as effective if you're set on playing small.

Don't get me wrong. If you want to stay small, be the best small business you can be. But I think that would be a mistake. Here's why:

Half or more of the money you will ever make from your business will come on the day you sell it.

Institutional investors go for big deals. The bigger, the better. If you're a small business, you'll have an incredibly difficult time cashing in on the asset you've created.

So, if you're going to stay small, you need to be willing to own that decision at every stage—including when you go to sell, and the size, lack of systems, or lack of management maturity prevents that sale. And the gut punch here is—it doesn't matter how much money, time, sweat, or energy goes into building your company. It's simply not a sellable asset.

Kenny, the co-founder of Kajabi, spent a full year coding Kajabi at night and on weekends to get the company up and running. For over a decade, Kajabi was

---

4   Gracious Quotes. "81 Charlie Munger Quotes on Life and Investing (WISDOM)." *Gracious Quotes*, December 2023. https://graciousquotes.com/charlie-munger/.

a proudly bootstrapped (and profitable) business. Without his diligence and determination to be bootstrapped, we couldn't have controlled our destiny.

But without an understanding of our market value or our exit strategy, we would have never ended up raising $550M in funding with a $2B valuation.

I've met many business owners who understand with expert competence every aspect of their business and industry. Unfortunately, the same entrepreneurs either don't know the worth of their company, or worse yet, have some number entirely detached from reality.

Do not be the business owner who leans solely on passion and enthusiasm. Don't let your passion become your purgatory, or worse, your punishment.

You can have the perfect brand, product, market opportunities, etc., and no investor or buyer is going to take a second look in your direction if you haven't achieved significant scale and profitability within your business. At the risk of sounding salesy, *that's why I'm writing this book.* To help you scale significantly using my proven strategy, the Bullseye Formula.

There is absolutely no point in playing small.

If you'd like, think of it through the lens of the common maxim, "Shoot for the moon and you'll at least land among the stars." Or, if you'd prefer my more direct view based on the data, there has never been a better time on planet Earth to build a business of meaningful size and scale. Global economies are larger and more mature, global opportunities abound in new and existing business categories, and the opportunity for you to have life-changing financial outcomes has never been greater.

According to Statista, global mergers and acquisitions amounted to approximately \$3.6T in 2021 alone.[5] If 80% of businesses in the United States are doing less than \$1M per year, then there's room for you to stand up, stick out, and shoot the lights out with your business.

How?

Keep reading.

5   Statista. "Number of Merger and Acquisition (M&A) Transactions Worldwide from 1985 to April 2023." *Statista*, 2023. https://www.statista.com/statistics/267368/number-of-mergers-and-acquisitions-worldwide-since-2005/.

How to Scale a Business Using the Bullseye Formula

Chapter 2

Ring #1: Purpose

Singleness of purpose is one of the chief essentials for
success in life, no matter what may be one's aim.

—John D. Rockefeller

The Purpose-Driven Center

I joined Kajabi as its president when we were at about $6M in ARR (Annual
Recurring Revenue) and around 25 employees. We were bootstrapped and
profitable.

Over the next five years, we built to north of $100M in ARR, had 400+
team members, and a beautiful 55,000-square foot office space next to the
Irvine Spectrum in Orange County, California. We went into Covid with 80
employees and exited it at over 400.

It was wild but relatively simple. Because our purpose was at the center of
our target.

We were fortunate. Not in the tactics we chose or the sudden need for online
platforms like ours (although, that did help!). We were fortunate because we
nailed our purpose right out of the gate.

You met Kenny in the Foreword. (If you skipped it, I'd recommend reading it
now and circling back.) Kenny's purpose in co-founding Kajabi was singular:
To create a world where entrepreneurs, thinkers, and creators like him could
connect their knowledge to the world.

When I joined Kenny, my purpose was less tangible but just as powerful: I saw the potential in Kajabi and knew that my experiences—both my successes and failures—had prepared me to help scale the business to the moon.

This is the first key piece of Purpose: Your internal driver. The mistake so many business owners make is to create mission, vision, and values for their employees at this stage. I'll speak more on this later, but for now, understand that this first part is about you—no one else. Nobody will sacrifice what you will, so you need a purpose so personal that it will drive you through every single barrier.

You could be Paul Orfalea, who sold Kinko's and once told me, "The business was for sale the day I opened the doors," because that was his purpose. Your purpose might be at the core of who you are and how you want to show up to the world. It might be connected to goals you have for your family. Or, it might just be that you want a ton of money. In my world of purpose, that's okay.

Fueling my purpose was the vision I had for my life dating back to my early days in college. A mentor of mine suggested I keep a journal—which I still keep to this day.

On April 27, 2001, I wrote:

Writing my thoughts down for my own benefit and leaving a legacy seemed like a good idea, so here we are.

(I know. My nineteen-year-old wit was astounding.)

In this particular entry, I went on to list my ideal day, down to the times I would wake up and go to bed, where I'd live, what my house would be like—"An extensive audio system will play music in every room"—and what kind of cars I'd drive. (Yes, cars.)

I may have been young, but I believed that what I wrote down would come to pass given the right circumstances. And it did, down to the last detail. (Well,

Dear Journal,   4/27/01

Where to begin? Writing my thoughts down for my own benefit, and leaving a Legacy seemed like a good idea; so here we are. My first year of college is

audio system will play music in every room, and the appliances will be Bang & Olafson. I'll have a large pool w/ elaborate waterfalls and a lucious yard. I believe 5000 sq. ft. will be sufficient.

– Cars...

I'll be driving a Twin turbo Porsche, alternating with a CL 600 and an s 600. The Porsche will be silver, the CL will be white and the S black.

my wife actually drives one of my "dream" cars; I decided to go with a BMW, so we're a house divided.)

It's important to understand the why *behind your why* if money is your internal driver. For me, the vision I journaled about represented fulfillment, achievement, success, freedom, and stability. It meant being a provider for my family and not being chained to a desk or beholden to someone else's whims or expectations.

All (or most) of the decisions I've made in life and business since that day in 2001 were informed by my internal purpose.

This is the second key piece of Purpose: Your external driver. This is not for your team; this is for your customers. External purpose is the problem you solve for them. This is your customers' why.

For Kajabi, we knew that providing users with a platform to sell their knowledge and serve their customers would not only provide life-changing education and skill acquisition for audiences but also life-changing incomes for our customers. Simply put, we knew Kajabi would make the world a better place. This end—our customers' success—was our external purpose.

Internal purpose: Why are you doing what you do?

External purpose: Why do you do what you do for the people you do it for?

The nuance between internal and external purpose is an extremely important distinction, and it's something a lot of businesses miss. You must have both to form a set of decision-making guardrails that not only keep you on the right track but also give you the fuel you'll need to persevere through the difficult seasons of scaling.

Now, when you ask yourself why you're doing what you do, be prepared for answers to surface that you know aren't real. Your first answers might be just to make money, live a picture book life, or be able to say "I did it" to that former lover, high school bully, or in-laws. If that's your real purpose, like I said, in my world of purpose, that's okay.

But dig a little. You might find a deeper purpose. Maybe "money" really means the long-term stability you never experienced growing up. Maybe it really means the respect of your family or peers. Maybe it really means an early retirement that allows you to be a more present parent or grandparent.

You must find a purpose that you are deeply connected to. It might stem from a pain you've experienced, an injustice you've witnessed, or something you're just stubborn about. To grow something big, your purpose has to run deep, or you'll find yourself waking up in the morning not remembering what's driving you. And when what's driving you isn't front and center, you end up getting distracted, changing your mind, and never getting the traction you need.

With that said, your internal driver will likely shift throughout your experience growing a business. With Kajabi, my purpose expanded over time. In fact, after a while, it was the external driver that became my internal driver. Seeing the transformative power of entrepreneurship in the lives of people who used Kajabi became an irreplicable motivator.

This is why it's okay to be real and raw with your internal purpose. It's hard to start thinking about serving the world when you're focused on rent and a car payment, but you'll find as you check those urgent and important personal boxes, your purpose will naturally shift to service when you're ready.

External purpose is like the horizon; you're always pointed in that direction ... but it's the internal purpose that gets you up each morning to row the boat.

What drove my purpose further wasn't even the stories of the users who said, "Yeah, I made a million dollars last year." It was people like Leah McHenry.

"I was homeschooling five children. I loved my music, and I couldn't go on tour because I was homeschooling my kids. But I learned how to use Facebook ads to sell my music, and I made enough money that I didn't need to go on tour. I figured other musicians would like to know how I did that, so I launched a business, made seven figures on launch, retired my husband who was in construction, and our first big purchase was a dining room that could seat 12 people because we had never had a table big enough for my five kids and any other family members."

Leah's gone on to have multiple successful enterprises.

Stories like Leah's began to shift my perspective and purpose. What started out as a journey to scale and exit big became a journey to help Kajabi users accomplish their wildest dreams and beyond. The power of that purpose drove us to heights we never imagined possible.

Your internal and external purpose will lead you in identifying your business's overall purpose, but the former two must come first.

I'm a very big believer that if your business does not have a purpose for existence, all of these other elements move you into a commodity category, and the company doesn't have a reason for existing. If you don't nail Purpose, this is going to be a perpetual problem, and it will affect every single ring in the Bullseye Formula.

When you have your internal and external purpose dialed in, you see something spectacular—the potential of what your business could really be. It's way off in the distance, and that abyss is the uncertainty of what scaling beyond a lifestyle business will look like.

You have the headaches you have now, and on the other side of scaling mode—you get the headaches you choose, **but you don't necessarily know the price of your success until after you've paid it.** You're going to have to be able to look into the abyss and do what it takes to get through it. This is where your purpose is most powerful.

Artist Versus Entrepreneur

If you want a purpose that is absolutely bulletproof, think of it this way:

Defining your internal and external purpose is the essential blending of the artist and the entrepreneur.

Artists create beautiful works of art in a dingy attic, often starving and unappreciated. They create what aligns with their internal purpose without great regard for what they think the public wants or needs. In fact, artists stereotypically get a kick out of being "misunderstood" by the masses.

Entrepreneurs, on the other hand, create for an audience. They find a problem and create a solution. They create what they are confident the public wants and needs, like Kenny creating a sprinkler toy and realizing that there was no solution for getting a digital product out to the world, with himself being the beginning of his audience.

So, are you an artist or an entrepreneur?

The most successful entrepreneurs—the ones who scale big—are *both*.

An artist creates because they want to create. They're putting their work out into the world and letting the world decide what they want to do with it. Whether they admit it or not, they're emotionally attached to the opinions people form about their work and take those opinions personally.

An entrepreneur is solving a problem that people will pay to have solved. They're dealing with a wide and varied, demanding, and vocal audience. What they deliver has to perform and be fit for purpose. It has to exceed expectations.

But that doesn't mean creating and growing your business isn't art. It is. It's the work of both an artist *and* an entrepreneur.

- Artists and entrepreneurs are both highly creative and original. We have to be, but an entrepreneur's "output" has to have value to a wide audience; an artist just needs an audience of one.
- As much as you might like the idea of hiding out on an island, an entrepreneur needs to be in the world to connect, collaborate, lead, and inspire.
- If you're building something big, you have to believe that you have more control than you think you have. The smaller your business, the less you need to control. The bigger you grow, the more you need to take on, knowing you can win.

- You've got to love risk, my friend. A lot of it. You're putting more than the thing you create into the world. You're putting your livelihood and that of everyone who bets on you on the line too.
- You've got to be flexible in your thinking, honest, and capable of adapting to change fast.
- You need a certain amount of emotional stability. Few things chase talent away faster than an entrepreneur ranting from a ledge.
- Above all, you have to be independent in your thinking. You're building something new, something different. By definition, what you've done hasn't been done before. "Common," as in "commonplace," thinking won't get you there.

Understanding these boundaries is critical because entrepreneurship is an art. Art is a creative endeavor. Creativity needs boundaries, and Purpose puts those boundaries in place.

The lines you draw for yourself with purpose prevent that insane sense of overwhelm that will, I promise, wake you up at 2 a.m. It will prevent the paralysis of your experience when you have too many options in front of you. When you narrow your field of possibilities, you get to focus your energy and develop ideas within very specific parameters.

Having those parameters in place will encourage creative problem-solving by forcing you and your team to think outside the box and come up with innovative, interesting, different, and original solutions.

The Pull Strategy

An associate of mine came to me a few years back and asked, "How do I recruit? How do I get my company culture right? What do I do?"

The majority of ways companies go about recruiting are all wrong.

Here's the issue. Everyone reads the same books that tell them to get their mission, vision, and values together, and then it's, "Get your team excited about your mission, vision, and values. That's where the magic happens!"

And if that were true, magic would happen everywhere because every single company has a mission, vision, and values. Every single company has all the machinations to try and hire the "right people." Every single company is desperately trying to get these employees enrolled in this vision.

But that approach is broken, and here's why.

To start, the idea that every business needs a mission, vision, and values set dates back to 1974. That was before …

Computers
Mobile phones
Email
GPS
The internet

This isn't breaking news, but the landscape of business, life, and the entire world has changed significantly in the last 50 years. But we're still looking at employee engagement and alignment the same. This is a problem.

How do I know?

The last Gallup report told us that only 32% of employees are "actively engaged" at work.[1] Quiet Quitting, the Great Resignation, and global burnout have ravaged our workforce, creating staffing challenges, stifling productivity, and exacerbating supply-chain delays introduced by Covid.

---

1   Hsu, Andrea. "America, we have a problem. People aren't feeling engaged with their work." *National Public Radio*, January 25, 2023. https://www.npr.org/2023/01/25/1150816271/employee-engagement-gallup-survey-workers-hybrid-remote.

And we're still standing on the crumbling foundation of how businesses worked in the '70s.

Workers today don't want to be told what's meaningful and valuable. Instead, they want to be invited to contribute to something they intrinsically find meaningful and valuable. Workers today need to feel compelled by your purpose, not commanded by your mission.

Mission, vision, and values in the way that we approach it today are a *push strategy*, not a *pull strategy*. A push strategy looks like either:

- An organization already has a mission, vision, and values. Someone is being hired on with very little buy-in to purpose because they just need a job. They're not going to care about your "why." They're just there to pay the bills and live their life.
- An organization doesn't have a mission, vision, or values. Perhaps the company is trying to create it as they're bringing people on board. The company will survey and co-create the mission, vision, and values with all of the team members, resulting in a diluted purpose. Every employee is going to have completely different experiences and agendas. This option leaves you with a diluted and bastardized mission, vision, and values to push buy-in from your team.

If you're constantly using a push strategy to get your team to buy in, you're building a business that will be almost impossible to exit.

Because you're either the only believer who co-created with employees, who diluted your purpose to the point of being ineffective, or you're the tyrant who forced it on everyone so that they don't care about it anyway. Either way, it's not going to achieve the goal you want it to. Either path goes poorly for everyone involved.

This is why your success with the Bullseye Formula hinges on your ability to publicize and promote your purpose.

I call this "purposing in public."

Purpose in Public

This allows you to show the world what you're doing, why you're doing it, and who you're doing it for—*and that becomes a methodology of attraction.* In other words, **a pull strategy.** It's talking about your why and your purpose, which allows people to raise their hand and say, "I really want to be a part of what this person's all about."

A pull strategy is the most transformative way to articulate, improve, and optimize both your internal and external purpose in business. A pull strategy lets the universe divide your prospects and delivers the people who should come to you because they identify with your purpose.

A push strategy isn't motivating, no matter how many inspirational speeches you give. Employees who are pushed in may never actually care at all about it.

Let people choose to engage with your purpose. Let people choose to be attracted to why you exist. For example, if you really dig what Elon Musk is doing and he asks you to board his rocket ship, you don't care what seat you're in.

That's the response you're trying to generate with a pull-based vision: "I don't care where I sit, I just want to be a part of *that.*"

In my experience, you simply cannot get employees engaged in a vision that prompts them to go above and beyond for your customer base unless they are pulled in, not pushed.

I bet you can think of a dozen companies that have taken the traditional approach of mission, vision, and values, and yet, they aren't successful, even after their third offsite "team building" session.

I promise you that using a pull strategy will be the biggest trend of entrepreneurship in the coming decade. It will surpass all other recruitment strategies. It answers your content questions and your culture questions, and it answers how to scale internally with systems that people are excited about.

And if no one is excited about it, if no one cares about your pull strategy, then that in itself tells you what you need to know. It checks your business before you spend money on developing a product or advertising.

Promoting purpose in the public eye is the best thing you can do to hit the Purpose target dead center.

The second best thing is to accept that the people who join you might be attracted to your purpose, but they will always, always have *their own* internal purpose. If they didn't, they wouldn't go home to their families at night. You are the beacon, no matter how dedicated your team is, so it's critical that you stay committed, attentive, and focused, which brings us back to your internal and external purpose.

Your business's overall purpose has to be bigger than you or there'll be no gravity, no attraction—no pull.

An amazing example of purposing in public was Salesforce in the earliest days of SaaS. Their purpose was simple—move software to the cloud, starting with CRM (which was all "on-prem," a fancy way of saying companies had their own servers onsite). They took purposing in public so far as to hold parades and protests against the waste generated by CDs/DVDs on which software was originally sold and installed. Now that's a commitment to public purpose![2]

Similar to entrepreneurs who don't understand what meaningful scale requires (and believe it's working for three hours in the morning after

---

2   Ramadan, Al, Dave Peterson, Christopher Lochhead, and Kevin Maney. *Play Bigger: How Pirates, Dreamer, and Innovators Create and Dominate Markets*. New York: Harper Business, 2016.

your ten-step, self-care routine, posting on socials, and collecting big-time checks), purposing in public will scare off the people who don't understand what they're getting themselves into. Purposing in public shows them that not every day is great.

When I talk about purposing in public, I'm talking about all of the **real** stuff. This goes beyond transparency. It's a full pulling-back-of-the-curtain and exposing every aspect of your why. It's uncomfortable but worth it. For the people who are considering your business, it's going to give them a tremendous amount of permission to make their choice. They can see nothing is hidden. You've shared the good, the bad, the ugly, and the downright messed up instances of entrepreneurship. They can see what you're doing right and what you're doing wrong. It allows people to self-select the role they can play in contributing to the external purpose of your business. They can see that your company is authentic, and it gives the best chance of a good hire because there's nothing held back.

Purposing in public is the most multifaceted, impactful move you can make. You are going to find out from members of your community (or future members of your community) if they actually care about what you're building. Does what you're building resonate with what drives results versus what you think drives results?

(Spoiler alert: Probably not. It's usually not what you think because you're too close to it, but we'll address how to build an extraordinary product in the next section.)

Purposing in public is not just for pulling the right team to you. Purposing in public will bring light to your company culture and vision for everyone, including you. Purposing in public is the greatest litmus test of anything and everything you will do in your business, and it's available for free. All it takes is effort.

Because of your purpose, there are lines you won't cross, people you won't work with, suppliers you won't deal with, ideas you won't explore, and even money you won't make ... because it doesn't match your purpose.

As you can see, when you have a purpose, boundaries are created that show you what you can and will do. They also show you what you can't and won't do.

I outright laugh when I hear an entrepreneur shoot down the idea of purposing in public. "I don't have time," or "I don't have to. I can still be successful without it." And the inevitable question is, "Well, how is business going for you?"

I never get a good answer to that question. It's always, "Well, we just spent a hundred grand on ads last month, and we're really close to breaking even." I can't even fathom how that disconnect is allowed to live in the business. You can "YOLO" six figures on an ad campaign, but sharing your purpose intentionally is too difficult? Really?

It's entrepreneurial junk food to think the next ad campaign is going to save you. That's not where the insights are. That's not where the wisdom is. I love ads as much as anyone, but only after the real work is done.

Tim Ferriss said, "Being busy is a form of laziness—lazy thinking and indiscriminate action."[3] That's exactly why purposing in public is going to shape your business for the better. It keeps you accountable. Otherwise, your only honest posts might say, "Didn't do anything today. Played a lot of Call of Duty. Hoping for the best."

You can't wake up on Monday morning hungover, covered in Cheetos dust, and expect to change the world. (Believe me, I've tried.)

If you're really authentic with your purpose, then it's self-correcting. You

---

3   Ferriss, Tim (@tferriss). 2022. "Being busy is a form of laziness—lazy thinking and indiscriminate action. Being busy is most often used as a guise for avoiding the few critically important but uncomfortable actions." Twitter, January 12, 2022, 12:33 p.m. https://x.com/tferriss/status/1481318414 824218632?lang=en.

can't help but succeed because you are the one who is accountable to your-self every single time you talk about your why. Purposing in public is the ultimate crucible of bringing the company, culture, and vision into stark, objective reality.

Purposing in public also allows you to engage with your haters, which quite frankly is an audience you may learn from. The most I ever learned about my failures in a new company was taking a step back and having a dialogue with someone who was really angry at me in the moment—and truly setting aside my views and stepping into their shoes.

In working with Kajabi, this moment came as we realized that our tech stack is their whole stack. If you're not familiar with the term, a "tech stack" refers to the digital tools and resources a business uses to operate. Many of Kajabi's users rely on our technology to run their businesses from top to bottom. In other words, if our email application has a hiccup, it's no small ordeal. It could ruin a user's day and even gravely affect their business.

We have had new employees come in who weren't accustomed to the pres-sure, so we'd have to share our purpose publicly with them. We weren't just talking about another email marketing tool with Kajabi. We were talking about people's ability to pay their rent. About their ability to go to the gro-cery store. About their ability to pay *their* employees. That's what we needed our engineers and customer service reps to understand.

A buddy of mine built a very successful enterprise email provider. One day, we were talking, and I shared how angry some of our users had gotten over an outage in our application. I said, "You know, what's it like for you when your email tool breaks for all the Fortune 500 companies you serve?"

He said, "I'll get an email or two, but I'll just discount their next invoice and they're happy."

The stark contrast between our experiences was laughable. For us at Kajabi, the stakes were just simply higher. We had people with pitchforks and torches in our front yards because our tech stack wasn't just *software*. It was *sustenance*. It truly was life or death for our customers' businesses, and it was with that level of empathy that we all had to approach our work.

The most significant foundational shifts you can make as an entrepreneur involve understanding your purpose, your actions, and your target audience.

Take Aim ...

The most successful businesses are those that have a clear purpose—a reason for existing that is a combination of both your internal and external purpose.

When you really break it down, Purpose is the foundation of perseverance and passion. When you have a strong purpose—whether that's saving the world, building the best platform to solve a certain problem, or making money—you'll stay motivated and focused no matter how many obstacles and setbacks you face.

Purpose provides direction and helps you make decisions. It opens the door to high-growth opportunities and shapes everything from how you use your money, to what products you develop, and how you treat your customers. It is the dead center of the Bullseye Formula for a reason!

Sharing a mission, vision, and values is *very* 1974. Position yourself strategically by purposing in public. Consider your why *and* your customers' why in every decision and at each inflection point.

Purpose is not a fixed concept. As you and your business grow and evolve, your purpose will grow and evolve. Go with that flow but think about it first. Is your reason for existing starting to change because there's a real, deeper purpose? Or is it changing because things have gotten "too hard" and you're looking for a way out?

If the best of everything was easy, everyone would do it. Don't chicken out just because your purpose looks too big.

Here. I'll go first.

JCron's Purpose Statements:

My internal purpose is to continue to explore my personal growth and love of entrepreneurship by investing/advising with owners who want to scale their business to an astronomical valuation (assuming they've passed the tacos and tequila test[4]).

My external purpose is to help owners maximize their greatest wealth asset, scaling to an exit that allows them to do whatever they want to do for the rest of their lives.

Now, it's your turn.

---

4   Kenny and I derived the term "tacos and tequila test" when we started meeting with potential equity partners. The idea was that we'd take all prospects out to tacos and tequila. If we ended the meal and decided we'd enjoy another lunch together, even if we weren't in business with them, then we were open to doing business with them. But if we left the lunch and wouldn't care for another lunch together, we passed on the deal, no matter what the offer was.

Time to See Where Your Dart Lands

DO THIS:

1. Work out your internal purpose with raw and complete honesty.
2. Understand the external purpose that drives you.
3. Combine those two purposes to derive an ultimate, overall purpose for your company's existence.
4. If you're not purposing in public, how can you start *this week*?
5. Then, ask this question: Does anybody care?
6. If not ... go back to step 1.

_____

_____

_____

_____

_____

_____

_____

_____

_____

_____

Take some time now to think about your purpose.

**Score zero for "not me" and five for "exactly me"
or anything in between.**

Statement	Score
You wake up every morning knowing exactly why you're building or want to build your business.	
You can easily and simply answer the question, "Why are you doing this?" in 15 words or less.	
When you state your purpose, people get it immediately.	
When you talk about what you do, people are excited and want to get involved—or at least carry on the conversation!	
Late nights, early mornings, weekends, and regular meals pale in significance when you're in the thick of building your business.	
You're clear about what you will and won't do. You aren't easily persuaded by someone else's idea of the direction you should take.	
When things are tough, you relish the challenge and, even if you don't know exactly what to do, you know you'll work it out.	
You find it hard to shut up about your business, and the people around you are okay with that because your drive is infectious.	
When you sit quietly, alone with your thoughts, the reason why you're building your business feels good and real.	
If you told your kids why you're building your business, they'd be excited about it too.	

If you score below 20

My personal request to you is to go back to the start of this chapter, read it again, and then take some time to work out your purpose. Without it, it's going to be impossible to hit the Purpose target.

If you score 21 to 35

This is okay. You've got a few things in place. Take a look at the statements where you scored yourself three or below and do the work. DO THE WORK! Without this first ring in place, everything else will be harder, if not impossible.

If you score 36 to 50

You're good to go. Your internal and external purposes are clear. You're in the zone of pull, not push. You're ready to move to the second target—Profit.

How to Know You've Hit the Purpose Target

Hitting the Purpose target looks like firing on all cylinders. You have momentum, you have growth, and you're actively scaling.

When I was with Kajabi, my internal purpose had me waking up early and staying up late, talking to my friends and family, and literally being so unbelievably excited and obsessed with what we were doing and what we were building that I couldn't help but ooze enthusiasm for what we were working on.

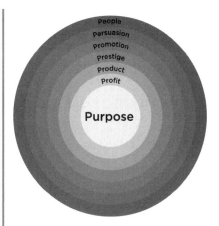

Figure 4 The Bullseye: Purpose

You need that type of internal purpose—**an internal purpose that is so powerful that the whole universe wants to rise up and conspire with you to help you achieve it.**

You'll know you're hitting your external purpose when, in talking about it, you see people leaning in with excitement and interest. You see people asking for information about how they can help or how they can get involved. You see people affirming that this is something your customers need—something the world needs.

You'll see people amped up enough to support, equip, or be enrolled in the vision that you're bringing forth for your customers. You'll see customers who want to refer other customers. You'll see customers want to put your logo on their computer, their car, their T-shirt, or their hat (Even a tattoo. No joke, our first customer support hire got a tattoo of the original Kajabi logo, you rock Omar!).

You've nailed external purpose when you begin to see something that becomes more than a business—it's a movement.

If you've realized, over the course of this section, that you need to recalibrate your purpose, don't panic. I understand it's daunting, especially if you're scaled and stuck. You might worry it's too late to consider Purpose. It's not. I came into Kajabi after it was already years into the game, and I'm deeply grateful for the partnership I shared with Kenny, who always kept us pointed toward our North Star and who was always willing to improve every area along the way.

How Purpose Ties to Profit

So far, we've talked about Purpose and why it's at the center of everything you do in business. Not because it's "nice" to have a purpose but because it directly impacts your profit.

On a personal level, if you don't have purpose, then you—as the owner—aren't going to care enough to get up and get after it day after day, which you absolutely will have to do if you want to scale big.

As an owner, your purpose may be to just sell for a ton of money. In my world of purpose, that's your choice and one I can relate to deeply. It doesn't matter what your purpose is. You just have to have one.

Without purpose, you'll have no pull. No magnetism. No real foundation on which to grow. And without that, you won't attract the right team, and your customers will treat you like a commodity.

If your purpose is to just have a cash-flow business, you might already have it. You might have delivered on it. You might not want to go through the work.

But, if what you're really saying is, "I want a category-creating, industry-defining business," you can't afford to miss a single ring on the dartboard.

So ... Get your purpose pinned down (accepting it'll change as you grow) and, with that in mind, turn your attention to the Profit target.

Chapter 3

Ring #2: Profit

Expansion is vanity. Profit is sanity. Overhead begs to walk on two legs.

—Felix Dennis

No Numbers, No Business. Know Numbers, Know Business.

The quote at the beginning of this section is by a poet named Felix Dennis, who also built a billion-dollar fortune from scratch. (Apparently, he had the artist/entrepreneur blend nailed.) His words remind me that profit is absolutely essential to any business. If you don't have profit, you don't control any aspect of your company. And if you don't control your company, how can you control your destiny?

Profit is the next ring in the Bullseye Formula because it is an essential support to Purpose. Without profit, you'll never fully actualize your purpose. Profit preserves the sanctity of your Purpose.

What I hope you take out of this ring of the Bullseye Formula is that if you don't have any measurable, profitable numbers, you have no business. In other words, you have to know your numbers to have a business with the ability and agility to scale.

Your numbers will teach you more about your business than anything else. No book on your shelf can give you clear guidance more effectively than knowing your numbers. It's actually shocking, and sobering, to see how many executives read voraciously, and yet never read and truly understand their own financial statements.

Some people can recite their top-line and bottom-line numbers. Even fewer people can say what typical employee fringe benefit rate is or what a fully loaded set of numbers are with allocations. (No idea what that means? Try a new example, like how to properly allocate variable or fixed costs.)

As you look at how your business scales, do you know how much it costs to acquire a new customer? Do you know what it costs to serve that new customer? Do you know what a new customer costs, by department, when you properly allocate all related costs?

If you're not looking at a fully baked set of numbers, you might think you're doing well and making up any losses with your volume only to find that your bottom line is less, your expenses are more, and now, you've got a whole set of headaches to deal with that you're not prepared for.

Look, you don't have to be profitable right away (though I think you should be). It can take time to get there. But do you at least have the confidence and certainty of when it will make money? You can't just grow and expect profit to follow.

The biggest mistake businesses make in this area is focusing on growth with no plans to make money or improperly managing working capital—because many people rely on loose financing to keep them afloat.

You can't do that. Immediately, out of the gate, you've got to know what your numbers are.

Never has this need for numerical clarity been more necessary than today. Depending on when you're reading this, we may be in boom times, bust times, or any varying degree of the times in between. I've met countless business owners confident in their enterprise value, describing it in big, round numbers that have a nice ring to them, only to see the business shredded in diligence (the fancy term for when an investor or buyer evaluates your business).

I've seen companies reliant on loose financing with a business model that equates to selling $100 bills for $20 and hoping that they can grow their way out of it in time. There is no shortage of economic calamities externally, and those you can't control, but the numbers I'm talking about you can control, and that's why they mean everything.

Your knowledge of your numbers will show how well you know your product, your systems, your customers, and ultimately, your business value. Without that knowledge, missteps of varying sizes are all but a guarantee. That's even more shocking when you consider that the net worth of most business owners is tied up in the value of their company!

It's safe to conclude, you cannot afford to be ignorant about the numbers in your business.

Ask yourself the purpose questions, and get yourself situated internally and externally. And then you have to immediately look at the viability of the business.

What are the numbers?

Don't hold back. This is a comprehensive exercise. Look at your business in terms of cost of goods sold, cost to deliver, cost to support, and true employee costs, including turnover! Every aspect of the financial equation needs to be solved for and clear.

Get those down and look beyond the numbers on your spreadsheet. Do those numbers work well enough to achieve what you're trying to do? Do the numbers work in favor of scale and delivery in terms of what profit means?

I can hear the objections already: "The SaaS world is different; those businesses are valued on a multiple of revenue. Profit doesn't matter, it's all about growth," (said the VC-backed tech crunch reader unaware of how businesses work). In SaaS, the **profitability is actually why SaaS companies trade on revenue multiples. (If you're in SaaS, please read that again**). SaaS gets that valuation based on the belief that at any moment the growth spend can be turned off and the net revenue retention flips the business to insanely profitable—assuming you built it right.

But even with every SaaS exception you'll try to argue, building with profit in mind will only help your odds of successfully selling your SaaS business.

And yes, I know there are those of you who want to rely on institutional capital to carry you over the hump and into glory. I'll get into this a bit later, but institutional capital is the wrong move for the majority of business owners seeking it. Stay bootstrapped and profitable—it keeps you honest. Institutional capital, if left unmanaged, makes you lazy more often than not.

What's more, investors don't walk around with an open checkbook. I have a friend who walks in and immediately looks at the equipment a business is using. If they've purchased the newest model of MacBook for every employee and brand new office furniture, he won't invest in that business. Period. End of story.

If you are considering investors for your business, you'll need your numbers in line. An investor will look at every aspect of your business to see whether it's even worth investing in before there's ever a discussion of how much money they're willing to put forth.

Being bootstrapped and profitable made all the difference in Kajabi's long-term success. This was all Kenny. As I've said, Kenny spent over a year coding before Kajabi ever went live. And during that year, he spent probably four to six months doing work for free for industry leaders with a beta version of Kajabi in order to build a waitlist for people to join the platform. Kenny called it "marketing to the front row."

I'll share more about this in future chapters, but know that this one decision meant Kajabi started with $1M in ARR (annual recurring revenue) on the day of its launch.

Kajabi never took on any debt, no institutional capital, nothing other than the investment of blood, sweat, and tears. (Or was it a clear strategy and purpose, long hours, unwavering dedication, and the right people?) Decisions were not made based on hope. Decisions were made based on how well something performed. Then, every dollar saved was a dollar that could be invested, that could be taken out of the business for lifestyle, that could be put wherever we wanted.

Kajabi's approach to profit allowed us to retain control of our vision and make decisions based on purpose. It allowed us to bet long-term. It allowed us the ability to remove temporary aberrations of the market from our business plan. Given the industry we were in, we knew if we were in it long enough, we'd win. Profit allowed us to call those shots and become very successful.

Now, that isn't to say that we always nailed the Profit target. Far from it. Initially, we didn't do nearly enough optimizing over the course of the business. Our first pricing strategy, which predated my involvement, was purely rectal extraction (technical term for pulled out of our collective posteriors). It was just looking at what the marketplace was charging and calibrating it accordingly. We were fortunate that the business metrics continued to work out.

In addition, we made the mistake of not having many expansion revenue opportunities within the company. That was another area that we should have planned better on the pricing side. We were the beneficiaries of having a business that had a lot of elasticity in pricing, and that's what allowed us to stay profitable. But our ultimate saving grace was that we consistently watched the numbers and stayed bootstrapped. We knew every month if the top line and the bottom line were working.

We have a far more sophisticated system now as a nine-figure company than we did as a seven-figure company. You can grow into that level of complexity, planning, and reporting, but at the beginning, always hold yourself accountable to the bottom line. Allowing your business to freely accelerate top-line results that effectively feed the bottom line is a foundational principle that ensures you're going to have a fighting chance.

Understand your numbers; don't underestimate their importance.

Ask yourself:

- When was the last time I looked at the numbers?
- How often am I reviewing them?
- Who is holding the business accountable according to the numbers?

And more importantly ...

Who has the power of the purse strings?

If you're not personally signing the checks, I promise you that there are checks going out that shouldn't be signed.

You cannot overestimate the importance of profit. It is an absolute essential.

Cash Flow Fixes Everything

"Cash flow fixes everything" is easy to say, and while true, it also covers a multitude of sins. If the business doesn't have cash flow, it's likely not a business. If the business has great cash flow, it may mean that it's being run well or that it's capable of far more and the false cash flow confidence is covering poorly run departments.

It does more than let you pay the bills on time—it removes pressure from the day-to-day running of your business, gives you space to try things out, allows for creative and ad hoc explorations into new solutions and ideas, and gives you the choice to take your team to lunch without wondering whether the check will bounce.

Bottom line—cash flow lets *everything* flow.

Negative cash flow puts blinders on you. You stop seeing potential. You stop seeing dangers.

The number one failure of small businesses is being under-capitalized. Profit gives you options.

Think about all aspects of the profit equation—don't start with a flawed model and look at growth through the lens of "I'll make it up in volume."

How to Make It Work

The key is accepting that it's not just about cash flow; it's also about how you put your money to work.

All money that comes into your organization must have a job. Every dollar. And it must do that job from Day 1. To make sure it can do that, all income must be allocated the minute it comes through the door. Ideally, this should be automated.

Set up your banking so money flowing in is automatically moved to different pots: OpEx, profit, tax, investment, R&D. You decide based on your business's needs. Make OpEx (which includes payroll), tax, and profit your top priorities.

Yes, I said tax. (Don't roll your eyes at me.) The number of times I've seen businesses land themselves in trouble through overspending because they wanted to make sure Uncle Sam didn't get anything is mind-blowing.

Plan your spending. Know how much profit you want to take from your business. Know exactly how much it takes to run and grow your business. Know how much tax to put aside and put it aside.

The peace of mind you will achieve from that basic planning will set you and your business free while laying the foundation to scale to the moon without a hitch.

At the risk of sounding redundant, it's all about the numbers. Know them. Understand them. Use them.

If you're telling me you've got a game-changing approach to selling widgets, my questions will be:

- What is the cost of producing the product? This includes both direct costs (materials, labor, etc.) and indirect costs (overhead, utilities, etc.).
- How much revenue does the product generate? This includes both the price of the product and the volume of sales, less discounts, rebates, returns, or any other applicable offsets to revenue. (Yes, there are accounting categories for these, but stick with the mental model for simplicity.)
- What is the profit margin on the product? This is the difference between the cost of production and the revenue generated expressed as a percentage.
- Are there any fixed costs associated with the product that need to be considered? For example, are there marketing or advertising expenses that must be factored in?
- What is the break-even point for the product? This is the point at which the revenue generated by the product is equal to the cost of fulfilling it.
- How does the profitability of the product compare to other products in the same category or industry?
- Are there any external factors that could affect the profitability of the product, such as changes in the market, competitors, or economic conditions?
- Are there any opportunities to increase the profitability of the product, such as by reducing costs, increasing the price, or expanding into new markets?
- How does the profitability of the product fit into the overall financial strategy of the company?
- Are there any risks associated with the profitability of the product, and if so, how can they be managed or mitigated?
- What is your capital strategy?

- Can you grow it in a way that you're comfortable growing it?
- And if not, can you get money from people who will give it to you?

Can you answer these questions?

I'll say it over and over again: Know your numbers.

Not knowing your numbers can kill your business dead in the water. Even with an adoring fan base. Even with a great product. There's a reason the Profit target is the second of the innermost, foundational rings in this framework.

Take the companies below as examples. These all had huge fan bases and great products, but then for various reasons, they stopped keeping up and went bust.

Companies That Missed the Profit Target

Toys "R" Us dominated the market in the 1980s and '90s. The company had a loyal following because of its massive selection of everything a kid would want: toys, games, plushies, you name it. But they didn't keep up with consumer trends and online shopping. Sales declined. Financial difficulties followed. They filed for bankruptcy in 2017 and shut their doors to their largest markets in 2018.

RadioShack was a haven for tech enthusiasts who wanted nothing more than to fill their shopping carts with gadgets and electronic goodness. Similar to Toys "R" Us, RadioShack struggled to keep up with changing consumer trends. They failed to capitalize on the growing demand for online shopping. As a result, they filed for bankruptcy in 2015 and closed most of their stores.

Blockbuster ignored the rising trend of online streaming and stuck with physical stores and DVDs. Once again, financial loss led to bankruptcy in 2010.

Borders disappointed their fans when they struggled to adapt to the rise of eBooks and online shopping. You can see the pattern ... declining sales, financial difficulties, bankruptcy in 2011. Borders no longer exists.

Heck, today the average lifespan of a Fortune 500 company is fewer than 18 years. Making that focus on cash flow critical when even the biggest of the big can be upended if that focus isn't maintained.

So ... cash flow is king! When you see your numbers dwindling, you have to look around you. You have to find out why. You have to adapt.

Ideally, you'll adapt enough to continue to grow, but you might decide you need outside capital to make that leap.

Accounting

We're going to talk about outside capital, but let's first finish a conversation on how you track your numbers. Official disclaimer: This is not a book on accounting. I'm most definitely not an accountant, and the purpose of this section is the strategy behind your reporting and how to equip you to build the reporting that is correct for your business. I highly recommend having the best CFO/CPA/finance team that you can hire, and we should've done this sooner at Kajabi.

With that disclaimer in mind, let's talk about cash and accrual accounting strategies. Cash accounting and accrual accounting are two methods used to track and report financial transactions. Let's quickly break down the two.

In cash accounting, transactions are recorded when cash is received or paid out. It focuses on actual inflows and outflows of dollars. This is often referred to as cash basis or tax basis accounting. Let's say you sold $1M of products in April but collected the payment in June. You would record revenue of $1M in June when you COLLECTED the payment, even though the products were sold in April.

Accrual accounting records transactions when they occur, regardless of when payment is exchanged. For instance, if you completed a coaching seminar in September for $20,000 but waited until November for payment, you would record the revenue in September for $20,000 when you performed the service, even though you had to wait two months for payment. Every business should start with cash accounting because it continues to hold you accountable to the numbers in the cleanest and easiest way possible, and it prevents financial cash flow mismanagement that can sometimes come with accrual-based accounting.

From a planning perspective, accrual-based accounting is able to tie revenue and expense to when it is delivered, which is very helpful. It gives an accurate view of how the business is working and will aid in future financial forecasting. However, early on, and without a great financial department to help you, accrual-based accounting can lead to a lot of cash flow issues because businesses may have to pay expenses earlier than the revenue is actually in hand.

For example, if you needed to buy a hosting package up front and you need to pay $10,000 for a year, due in January, but you're accounting shows you are paying 1/12 of that amount over the course of each month, you might be wondering why you're accounting says you're profitable, but your bank account says you have no money.

I recommend both a cash and accrual accounting method ... eventually. Start with cash, and once you have the help you need to manage accrual accounting, use them both in tandem.

Is Outside Capital Right for You?

Now let's tackle a much-debated topic: outside capital. Nine out of ten times, raising capital is not the move for you.

And if you're going to raise money, you better know why you want it, and you better be prepared for everything that comes with it.

Institutional capital (venture capital, private equity, merchant banks, or institutional funds) gives you the impression that you're smart. Before you know it, you've blown $10M on stuff you would have never bought. That capital covers a plethora of seemingly smart, yet entirely unnecessary decisions—like an office suite you can't really afford. It can make you a lazy entrepreneur because you're not held to the same standard as when every dollar has to sing for its supper.

If raising capital is a serious consideration for you, pay close attention here.

The reasons to raise capital are:

1. I have no money and no ability to generate a minimum viable product without at least some money. (And I've exhausted friends and family, personal savings, side hustles, etc.)
2. My idea requires highly skilled and uniquely educated professionals, (think medical devices or aerospace), without which I cannot launch the business in any form.
3. My idea is so big, so game-changing or time-sensitive, and subject to a binary-style land grab that without a war chest to win, I'm dead in the water.

Take a look at the competitive research for your idea. If you believe you are staring down the barrel of a land grab, that if you do not actualize that opportunity faster than everyone else around you, you'll lose it, then raising capital is a good move for you.

Is the idea you're capitalizing on perishable? If so, who else is capitalizing on it and what situation are they in? If they have already raised money, is your idea that much better? And can you sell investors on why it's better?

Stripe and Braintree are perfect examples of why you would choose institutional capital. Because merchant services are a zero-sum game, and speed to market is a significant advantage, Stripe became the market leader. They raised a whole lot more capital than Braintree, which allowed them a different path. So, if you want to own a similar market, you'll need the capital to get there bigger, faster, and better than everybody else.

In other words, if your strategy is to get big faster than organic growth will support, and there is no alternative, then raise capital.

If your strategy is to be unbelievably excellent and control your destiny (which is what I believe almost every company should do), then don't raise any money. The constraint of not having dumb money will force you to be a better entrepreneur and a better business owner. And you'll make far more money in the long run.

The Little-Known and Often-Overlooked Factors in Raising Capital

There's a personal buy-in when raising capital (aside from the dollars in your bank account funding the preliminary aspects of your business).

You have to ask yourself:

Am I personally prepared to raise capital?
Am I personally prepared to have partners who may question
my moves and decisions?
Am I prepared to be held accountable to a board of financial wizards?
Am I prepared to be on a treadmill that is turned up as fast

as it possibly can go?

Do I believe my business can get big enough to deliver the returns investors want?

And, am I prepared to run a business that way?

Am I ready for direct feedback and oversight from new partners?

Raising capital isn't just a snapshot of what you see on *Shark Tank*. A good story, a researched product, and killer marketing aren't the only propelling factors here. It's a full-time job. You're in the business to raise money, burn it down, then lather, rinse, and repeat—ad nauseam.

That's the job you have. It's not just growing the company; it's now also raising money. Don't forget that. Growing the company is still required.

Forewarning, it's like a drug. The first time you get an investor to promise a heap of cash for your business capital, it will be the greatest high ever. And then you have to chase that high in bigger and bigger rounds to keep your company growth goal. The hope is that you pull it off and do it right ... but your capital will be the fuel that either takes the rocket to the moon or explodes it on the launchpad.

Venture capitalists take moon shots only. So, if your style is slow and steady wins the race, then you picked the wrong partner, and they're going to burn you out.

If you're in a high-growth business that has a massive burn rate, things get intense and chaotic. You can expect long hours with little to no weekend or holiday breaks because you are desperately trying to outgrow whatever the requirements are for your next fundraising round.

This is where your CEO role will look entirely different than anything you expected when starting your business. You'll have the personal challenges of dealing with somebody else's schedule, timeline, or goals that may not be yours or may not be what's best for the company.

Things that were entirely your purview, no questions asked, are now fielded by smart individuals who have put a lot of capital into your business with a desire and ability to influence its direction. Be prepared for more leadership voices at the table that you must answer to first—ahead of your customers.

Your decision-making power changes when you accept working/venture capital. The decisions are not, "What's the best thing for our customers?" It's, "What growth numbers do we need to show to get the next check?" because your business is now run by projections and budgets.

If you, as an entrepreneur, have a hunch, you'll likely need permission to go after that hunch unless it's in the budget. You have to qualify decisions with a board of investors that would otherwise be left to your discretion if you bootstrapped your business.

Add all of this to the fund life—the timeline of what your fund has committed to its investors. If investors were told they would earn their money back in five years, be prepared for somebody to tell you to sell, to get another investor to take their position, or to tell you that you'd better IPO. The fund life adds a ticking clock to your business growth that you have no control over.

Moving Ahead with Capital

If you're at this point and raising capital seems like your natural next step, a capital provider is going to want to say, "Hey, congratulations! You have a good idea, but how much do you know about the rest of it?"

What is your total addressable market? What are you bringing to that market that's differentiated? What are your financial projections of what it's going to cost you? What's your growth rate, and can you grow faster than others and maintain it? And assuming you do it well, how much is it worth?

And they won't stop there. If you think buying a house or having a colonoscopy is invasive, just ask professional investors for capital.

There are an additional six benchmarks I advise you to have in hand before exploring institutional investment:

1. **A strong team, particularly in finance and management.** Institutional investors are not interested in operating your business. Before turning to funding, make sure you have followed the rings of the bullseye to set up strong systems and a team to support those systems, even if you're still considered a "small" business when obtaining funding. In addition, after getting funding, your financial reporting requirements will expand exponentially—be ready, get a jumpstart on the process, and have your financial information audited (or at least reviewed).

2. **An established, diversified customer base.** Meaning, your mom isn't keeping you afloat with 50% of your yearly sales. In order to be an attractive and easy option for investors, make sure no single customer accounts for more than 20% of your sales. Customer diversification reduces investor risk.

3. **A profit margin on par with industry averages.** More is better in this category. A high profit margin can afford to make a few mistakes and still make money. Investors don't care about your purpose. They don't care about your vision. This is a mutually beneficial situation that has everything to do with cold, hard cash.

4. **A strong, competitive difference.** Investors want to know that your company can survive the long haul. If you're like any other highly commoditized business, it's a crowded race to the bottom. Competitive differentiation is difficult to replicate and thus protects your growth and your position in the market.

5. **A product or offer that isn't too trendy or dependent on cycles.** Right in line with competitive differentiation, you have to be able to prove that your business provides a relatively consistent product.

6. **A clear line to profitable growth, keeping in mind that not all growth is profitable.** Increased profits mean increased business value, which ultimately makes your investors more money.

Having capital isn't a silver bullet. It doesn't last forever. There's a point when the tide goes out, and we see who's swimming without their bathing suit.

Smart, informed decisions will keep you dry, or at the very least, clothed. And the Bullseye Formula is designed to do exactly that.

It's all in the numbers and that's good news. If you had to make critical business decisions on anything else, you'd be hit or miss. When you track numbers, you can't con yourself that an okay idea is incredible.

Essentially, you track the Level One numbers. These numbers must be tracked with clinical accuracy. I call them "Level One" because they're likely the best place to start.

1. **Revenue:** The total amount of money that a business generates from sales. Tracking revenue is crucial for any business, as it provides insight into how much money is coming in and can help identify growth opportunities.
2. **Gross profit margin:** The percentage of revenue that remains after deducting the cost of goods sold (COGS). A high gross profit margin indicates that a business is efficiently managing its costs and generating a healthy profit from its sales.
3. **Net profit margin:** The percentage of revenue that remains after deducting all business expenses, including COGS, operating expenses, and taxes. A high net profit margin indicates that a business is generating a healthy profit after accounting for all costs.
4. **Cash flow:** The amount of cash that is coming in and going out of a business. Positive cash flow is essential for a growing business, as it ensures that there is enough money to cover expenses and invest in growth opportunities.
5. **Return on investment (ROI):** The return that a business earns on its investments, such as marketing campaigns or new equipment. Tracking ROI can help businesses identify which investments are generating the most value and which ones may need to be reevaluated.

There are other numbers that businesses forget to track because it takes effort. Remember, we want to grow your bullseye. Knowing your numbers is how you'll master the Profit target, an essential ring in expanding your bullseye.

These are the Level Two numbers. And when I say Level Two, I don't mean less important, I mean they're a little more buried and might take some work to get right. But as you can see, they're critical.

- **Accounts receivable turnover:** This metric measures how quickly a business is collecting payment on its outstanding invoices. Tracking accounts receivable turnover is important for maintaining healthy cash flow and ensuring that customers are paying their bills on time.
- **Inventory turnover:** This metric measures how quickly a business is selling its inventory. Tracking inventory turnover is important for managing inventory levels, minimizing waste, and ensuring that products are selling as expected.
- **Debt-to-equity ratio:** This metric compares a business's debt to its equity and helps determine how much of a company's assets are financed through debt versus equity. Tracking this ratio is important for maintaining a healthy balance between debt and equity and ensuring that a business is not overleveraged.
- **Customer acquisition cost (CAC):** This metric measures how much it costs a business to acquire a new customer. Tracking CAC is important for understanding the cost of acquiring new business and ensuring that marketing and sales efforts are generating a positive return on investment.
- **Lifetime customer value (LTV):** This metric measures the total value of a customer over the course of their relationship with a business. Tracking LTV is important for understanding the long-term value of customers and making strategic decisions around customer acquisition and retention.

Then finally, there are the Level Three numbers. Vital to understand, but often way too buried for the average business owner to uncover.

- **Customer retention rate:** This metric measures the percentage of customers who continue to do business with a company over time. Tracking customer retention rate is important for understanding customer loyalty and identifying areas for improvement in customer service and retention efforts.
- **Lead-to-close ratio:** This metric measures the percentage of leads that result in closed deals. Tracking the lead-to-close ratio is important for evaluating the effectiveness of sales and marketing efforts and identifying areas for improvement in the sales process.
- **Employee turnover rate:** This metric measures the percentage of employees who leave a company over a given period of time. Tracking employee turnover rate is important for understanding employee satisfaction and identifying areas for improvement in company culture and retention efforts.
- **Profit per customer:** This metric measures how much profit a business generates from each customer. Tracking profit per customer is important for understanding the profitability of different customer segments and identifying opportunities to increase profitability through pricing and product offerings.

All this leads to the big question ... How do I price my product so all these numbers (in the context of scaling my business) make sense?

A meticulously crafted pricing strategy is essential for achieving your dream exit. Pricing ranks among the foremost tools a business can employ to boost its valuation significantly, and is often the most neglected growth lever.

Don't wait until you're ready to sell before you set a pricing strategy—get that in place from the start. You won't get it right off the bat. Experiment with different pricing models and pricing strategies to find the one that maximizes profitability and growth potential.

The foundation of all pricing strategies is to understand the value that a business provides to its customers. Don't throw your business away by joining the race to the bottom and trying to undercut your competition. There's a reason they're cheap. Price based on your value. And if what you offer isn't of value to your customers, then change what you offer.

It's ALL about value-based pricing. Focus on pricing your products and services based on the *value* they provide to customers.

Frank Slootman (legendary tech CEO) believes that value-based pricing is essential for achieving sustainable growth and profitability.[1] He suggests that businesses should focus on understanding the specific pain points and needs of their customers, and then price their products or services in a way that addresses those needs and provides clear value.

In an interview with *Forbes*, Slootman explained that Snowflake's value-based pricing strategy has been a key driver of the company's success. He noted that Snowflake's pricing model is designed to align the company's incentives with those of its customers and to ensure that customers only pay for the value that they receive.

Overall, Slootman emphasizes the importance of focusing on value-based pricing, rather than simply trying to compete on price alone. By understanding the value that they provide to customers and pricing accordingly, businesses can position themselves for long-term growth and success.

Value-based pricing at Kajabi was always a huge part of our profit strategy, both from a proposition perspective and a pricing perspective. The proposition perspective was one of simplification. Rather than our customers managing tons of tools, we figured it would be easier if all of the tools they needed were already in one place, integrated, and ready to go out of the box to drive results.

---

1   Lynley, Matthew. "Cloud Computing's Favorite New Business Model Is Starting to Look Like a Huge Risk as Markets Sour." *Business Insider*, May 2022. https://www.businessinsider.com/consumption-based-pricing-snowflake-cloud-companies-risky-market-downturn-2022-5.

There are always inherent risks if you are the lowest price or the highest price. Ideally, for institutional investors, you want to have a strategy that allows for meaningful pricing growth over time that is consistent with value-based pricing for your customers.

The way that we showcase the value-based pricing is through comparison. We simply list what it would cost to buy each feature we offer separately— hosting services, web design services, email marketing provider, landing page provider, marketing automation provider, and digital product. All of those pieces combined are about 10 times the cost of Kajabi on a monthly basis. That positioning demonstrates a savings of 90% (and a lot fewer headaches) to our customers. It becomes a no-brainer.

Take Aim ...

Generating profit is the ultimate goal of any business because it lets you grow, expand, and ultimately, exit well. Profit gives you options. Any and all businesses need an emphasis on the Profit ring. Too many companies boast about what their value is while missing the only goal of all business—profit.

Effective cash flow management is critical. Keeping an eye on your money means you always have enough to do what you want to do, and what you have to do. Your profitable business can get into a cash crunch if you're not watching how the cash flows, hence the value of both cash and accrual financials.

At all costs (pun intended), avoid debt unless you know with absolute certainty that the debt will give you a return you couldn't achieve without it. The borrower is always beholden to the lender.

Everything your business does must generate recurring revenue. That predictable, growing, recurring revenue is what will keep you scaling. It doesn't matter whether that be subscription-based services, memberships, re-orders, or other recurring revenue models. Make sure your customers are worth more to you year after year.

For that to happen, you have to innovate. People won't pay for the same thing year after year unless it suits their purposes entirely. Even then, if a new player enters the field who does deliver the same thing you do, along with a whole heap of bright, shiny, extra stuff, your customers are going to take a look and then take a leap.

Always look for new ways to improve your products, services, and processes. Good news—your customers will tell you what they want from you, so simply listen.

And while you're doing that, pay attention to your money. How it flows, how it grows, and where you put it.

Time to See Where Your Dart Lands

DO THIS:

1. Get real about your numbers. Make a plan to review all your Level One, Two, and Three numbers in the next seven days.
2. Make sure every dollar has a job to do and automatically put your money to work the moment it comes through the door.

Time to think about your numbers. Be honest here. Conning yourself won't get you anywhere.

Score zero for "not me" and five for "exactly me" or anything in between.

Statement	Score
You know exactly how much it costs to get a new customer.	
You know exactly what it costs to serve that new customer.	
You know what a new customer costs you in the allocations of all of the departments that they're going to touch in the business.	
Even if you aren't making a profit now, you know with confidence and certainty when it will.	
You know (bullsh*t aside) what your company is worth.	
Your numbers aren't just on paper. Real and accessible cash is in the bank.	
When you look at your numbers in reality, you know with certainty they will let you achieve what you want to achieve in terms of scale and delivery.	
You review your numbers in full at least quarterly.	
You are the one who signs the checks.	
You are committed to bootstrapping your business so you can stay free and independent.	

If you score below 20

Don't mess around with this. If you don't know your numbers when you're at $5M, the chances of you scaling to $10M, $100M, or beyond are slim to none. Make the Profit target a priority. It gives you a choice while you run your business and the choice to sell it if and when you want to.

If you score 21 to 35

Mid-score is okay, but not good enough. Take this seriously and take it personally. It's not enough that "someone" in your business knows your numbers. *You* have to know them. Pay attention to anything you scored less than four on and make the needed changes.

If you score 36 to 50

You're running a business ready to grow. If you scored high for the Purpose target and high in the Profit target, you're ready to focus on your product.

If you didn't score high on the Purpose or Profit rings, you can keep reading, but don't try to "fix" anything until you've sorted out your foundational rings: Purpose, Profit, and the thing we're going to talk about next ... Product.

How to Know You've Hit the Profit Target

Hitting the Profit target comes down to a distinct decision that will stem from your purpose:

Is price your differentiator or is price your profit-enabler?

What I mean by that is choosing a price that is an advantage because it's lower than the competition's. If you have the ability to deliver on it without diluting the experience or disadvantaging your customers, this can be a powerful differentiator. However, if you're pricing lower in hopes of simply being able to get more volume, you may find yourself without a lot of profit to go around.

Figure 5 The Expanded Bullseye: Purpose and Profit

For me personally, my purpose would compel me to have a premium offering and a premium price that results in premium profits. Louis Vuitton is a perfect example of this strategy. As Bernard Arnault says, "[Luxury goods] is the only area in which it is possible to make luxury profit margins."[2]

I would encourage you to ask: "What's the best possible offering I can create and the best possible outcome I can deliver?" Then, price accordingly. If you've got a premium price, you've got room for profit.

Hitting this target and doubling the size of your bullseye is designing your profit strategy in a way that you're able to provide what you want, to the audience you want, and provide it in the way that you want, delivering on your purpose.

---

2   Quoteswise.com. "Bernard Arnault Quotes." *Quoteswise.com*, n.d. http://www.quoteswise.com/bernard-arnault-quotes.html.

For example, Walmart is the low-price leader—that is their purpose, their focus is on "EDLP"—everyday low prices. Their goal is to allow you to save money and live better by always having the lowest price, no gimmicks, no big discounts or BOGOs, just the cheapest price every day. That's Walmart. Louis Vuitton is delivering on a completely different purpose, and they're pricing and profit strategy reflects it. Both of them work.

In short, **hitting the target of Profit is profitability that aligns with your purpose.**

Let's be honest—it's impossible for me to speak directly to what nailing Profit would look like for you unless we were to sit down together and evaluate all your numbers. Depending on your business, I may do just that.

In the meantime ... Keep reading!

How Profit Ties into Product

Profit protects the sanctity of your purpose.

Without profit in your business, compromise comes knocking really fast. You start cutting corners or you have to borrow from people whose agenda doesn't exactly line up with yours.

Having the Profit ring fully operational supports your purpose. It is also what makes achieving product success possible. Profit is in the wrapper of the foundational rings, the glue that holds your fundamentals together. And if your product checks all of the boxes, then it exponentially increases the profit potential of your business.

As we move from Profit to Product, it's essential to understand how these fundamentals work in tandem to strengthen the core of your business.

And it's quite straightforward, but easily missed in the chaos of early business building.

You have to sell something people want in order to make any money.

What is often misunderstood is the exchange of value a business presents to its customers. Go way back in ancient history to a civilization that didn't have currency. How did their economics work? Bartering. Exchange. I have these delicious apples from my family farm. You have warm pelts and coats. Let's trade.

We fool ourselves into thinking our way of life is more sophisticated than that.

It isn't. All we're doing is exchanging resources. Our currency, time, and energy are all resources we use to build what we can and exchange for what we want or need.

Understanding this principle begs the understanding behind pricing. You can't jack up a price if the demand isn't there. It'll implode your business from the inside out if you price your product too cheaply to keep existing.

Business is an exchange. Profit and Product are contingent upon that exchange.

We'll get more into the nitty gritty of Product in the next section, but I'd like to plant a few seeds ahead of time so you can reap valuable lessons when we revisit these concepts in the third ring:

1. Consider the cost of production or outsourcing. This isn't to act as a deterrent but will inform your pricing strategy and affect the overall longevity of your business.
2. Price too high and you won't have a customer base to support your business. Price too low and you'll cannibalize your company before dinner.
3. Quality. Are you providing a transformational experience? This creates a network effect you cannot replicate any other way, and it will grow your business more effectively than any marketing or sales strategy ever could.

With those nuggets on Product, let's dive in.

Chapter 4

Ring #3: Product

Any product that needs a manual to work is broken.

—Elon Musk

Good Products Are Hard to Find ... and Even Harder to Create

Let's say that tomorrow morning the government outlaws sales and marketing in all forms. Can't run ads. Can't use salespeople. Can't build funnels.

What happens to your business? What happens to the cash flow?

Does your company churn out in three months, leaving you with nothing left?

Does your business stay flat because there's no net dollar retention or expansion opportunities other than new customers?

Does your business slowly peter out over time because you got to a market early, you've got some great, golden handcuffs, and there are no alternatives yet?

Or does the business continue to grow because every dollar this year is worth $1.20 the next year?

Not only is this last example a great company to run, but it is the most likely company to sell for a big multiple.

As unlikely as a total marketing shutdown is, you can future-proof your business and nail your Billion Dollar Bullseye trajectory by focusing on your product.

This is the last of the three core rings that make up the center rings of our bullseye. Purpose, Profit, and now, Product are of foundational importance to your venture.

And you'll know you've nailed your product when you almost can't constrain the growth. The referral engine, love engine, impact engine … you've nailed your product when you can't stop people from wanting your product or buying it.

Brian Chesky of Airbnb, said, "Build something a hundred people love, not something a million people kind of like."[1] This is a lens on business that entrepreneurs avoid the most because, for many, your product is your baby. And nobody wants to hear that their baby is ugly.

Once a product is created, we tend to reevaluate and iterate every single part of our business *besides it.*

But Product is the single best lever you can possibly find.

Be warned, having a good product is incredibly hard.

This is why business owners go to every conference imaginable to find the ultimate social media ad hack, the next sales funnel, or the supercool whiz-bang AI that builds your business for you.

If this resonates with you, whatever fix you're searching for, odds are it's because you don't want to look at your product with an objective set of eyes and ask if it's really doing what it's meant to do.

---

1   Shontell, Alyson. "The Best Advice Airbnb CEO Brian Chesky Ever Received." *Business Insider,* June 2013. https://www.businessinsider.com/the-best-advice-airbnb-ceo-brian-chesky-ever-received-2013-1.

You have to be willing to go through all the iterations and the process that comes with building a game-changing product. This is where most owners fall short. They don't want to take the time or energy and experience frustration or impatience to create the kind of product that would sell without marketing.

Instead, they compromise on their product. They deliver a half-baked, so-so, gets-the-job-done product that only slightly satisfies their customer base and then throw a hyped-up marketing funnel married with a high-pressure sales process behind it to actually sell.

You'll see this type of marketing displayed everywhere. Some call it *bro-marketing*—a term used to describe hype machines driven by affiliate partners all promoting each other's get-rich/skinny/smart-quick products. You know the products and the companies. It's the pitch that something clearly significant in accomplishment and scope can be achieved from your couch if only you knew the secrets they know and bought the tools they are selling.

There is a reason that businesses powered by bro-marketing never sell—because they're not legitimate businesses. They're marketing campaigns. They're loosely organized collections of income or health claims, powered by hype, with no value to be conferred.

There were two different instances at Kajabi when our marketing team, very pleased with their numbers, said, "Our ads are crushing it. Look at our ROAS (return on ad spend)!" We didn't quite buy it.

In one of those instances, we hired a very professional ad buyer who was spending big money in a variety of places and experimenting with different types of ads. We had also brought in a supposed expert in analytics who was providing all of the attribution, spreadsheets, tracking, and codes necessary to see where sales were coming from.

The decision to turn off advertising in this case was a very difficult one. It felt like we were saying, "Hey, we appreciate your effort, but we're just not sure it's effective." That's not fun to say *or* hear because it's difficult for people to separate their effort from their effectiveness. But because we were serious about our profit target, it was a conversation we were willing to have.

This is a time when, in Kajabi's universe, it became critical to be data-informed and not data-driven. If we were data-driven, we would have stayed with the spreadsheets and continued to spend ourselves into oblivion. Instead, we took a hard look at our data—at the ad spending—and we asked, "Do we really feel like the results of these ads justify these numbers?" The answer—we weren't sure.

Over a series of meetings, we used experience, knowledge, and good old-fashioned intuition to determine that the ads weren't converting at a level that the spending would dictate. This was where being a profitable company gave us a lot of latitude because we knew that if we turned off the advertising and we were wrong, it'd be okay to miss a little bit of growth— we'd just double down on ad spending the next month.

But if we were right, we were going to save a ton of money.

Because we were bootstrapped, we were able to make that decision internally. Then, after a big, deep breath, we turned off the advertising and watched it for a month. Lo and behold, our growth rate remained steady, and it completely changed how we were allocating dollars, time, and effort.

All said, we saved nearly $1M in ad-spend, and the product powered the growth anyway. We knew then that we had nailed the Product target.

We'll get more into the marketing side of things later, but for now, understand that your marketing should amplify an already incredible product. Good marketing will multiply what your product does on its own, but the product needs to be good enough to stand on its own.

And, by the way, if you're venture-funded out of the gate, you're accustomed to the fact that you've already sold people on your product being the greatest thing since sliced bread. You don't ever have that inflection point of considering the product you're holding and asking, "How successful can this be?"

And then the kicker, "What do I need to do to actualize its potential?" It's very unique to bootstrapped company owners because you'll often find that you're in varying degrees of a product/market fit. If you've nailed the product/market fit, your company will realize the promise of exponential growth only possible with an incredible, fully designed product.

Power of the Network Effect

One of my favorite authors, M.J. DeMarco, talks about the idea of product effectiveness in his book *The Millionaire Fastlane*: "Whereas a meritocracy pulls power to the skilled, a productocracy pulls money to the value of creators and businesses who grow organically through peer recommendations and repeat customers, compelled by a distinguished product and service not readily offered elsewhere ... your product contagiously sells itself."[2]

Let's look at an example through a SaaS lens with a company we're already familiar with: Kajabi.

As we've mentioned, Kajabi was coded by Kenny over the course of a year with no customers. It even started without an audience and wasn't publicly built or available. Kajabi then went out to three industry icons who were launching products and offered them a deal: Kajabi would handle the launch for free, and do everything, as long as the launch and product were built using Kajabi's platform. They even made sure there was a "powered by Kajabi" icon on the bottom of the page prompting viewers to sign up for a waitlist.

The waitlist grew exponentially. Pay attention to this—Kajabi launched as a $1M ARR (annual recurring revenue) company when it was publicly

2   DeMarco, MJ. *The Millionaire Fastlane: Crack the Code to Wealth and Live Rich for a Lifetime.* Highland, Utah: Viperion Publishing, 2011.

available on its first day. That is incredibly rare in software—incredibly rare in any business to be profitable on a recurring basis on day one!

How do you replicate that result? With the **Network Effect** created within a well-designed product.

Kajabi had a network effect that was so unbelievably spectacular, born out of how the company was originally launched, and carried through how the company grew in its category.

It had an element of the snowball effect where students from the original courses launched by those industry icons started to ask themselves, "How could I use this? What could I teach? What course would I offer?"

By simply exposing potential users to the product, Kajabi started a virtuous cycle within their product dynamics, and this is why the product is an absolute necessity in a successful business.

Power of Net Dollar Retention: A David and Goliath Case Study

Let's look at how powerful your product is when we look through yet another lens: net dollar retention.

Have you ever heard of a company named Figma? It's marketed as a "collaborative interface design tool." It's super cool, and the company essentially ate Adobe's lunch.

In fact, Figma was competing with Adobe so well that Adobe had no choice but to buy Figma for the biggest nosebleed-multiple ever offered in one of the worst technology environments in recent history. (Though the deal was killed due to antitrust regulations, the example is every bit as valid.)

Adobe wasn't dumb. It was a great choice—the only choice. They bought Figma because they understood basic math.

Figma crossed $400M in annual recurring revenue (ARR) at the end of 2022, up 100% from 2021 when it hit $200M in annual recurring revenue. In 2021, Figma more than doubled from $75M in 2020.[3]

The exponential nature of net dollar retention compounds year after year, eventually causing competitors' irrelevance in the market. Figma's net dollar retention was so good that, if left unchecked, the compounding effect would have eventually eaten Adobe alive. The network effect, or referral effect, was too powerful. Adobe couldn't get around it, so they did the smart thing and bought Figma instead of waiting to become a casualty of modern business economics.

What degree of confidence do you have that the dollar you get today is worth a dollar-plus tomorrow? That the client you get today is worth more to you tomorrow?

I ask because this is probably one of the biggest misses we had at Kajabi. They say the higher you climb the ladder of success, the more of your bottom the world will eventually see ... Here's ours.

In SaaS, net dollar retention should include upgrading your account and adding bandwidth, email volume, users, etc., incrementally increasing your plan level. As I mentioned in the profit section, Kajabi had near zero opportunities for this type of expansion, something Kenny and I grew to both rejoice and regret.

The rejoicing came from the net dollar retention shortcoming being a reflection of our purpose, our True North, namely, solving for the customer. Lacking opportunities for expanding revenue meant that more customers could enjoy additional features at no extra cost.

From a purpose perspective, this was good!

3   Sacra. "Figma." *Sacra*, 2022. https://sacra.com/c/figma/#:~:text=At%20the%20time%20of%20 Adobe%27s,and%20150%25%20net%20dollar%20retention.

The regret portion came from not accounting for what the success of our customers would eventually cost us. We had a few customers, who shall remain nameless, that cost the company roughly 20x more to support than they paid in subscription revenue. You read that right. We had some customers paying us $997 a year that, on video hosting and bandwidth alone, was costing us over $20,000 a year.

This is why Profit comes after Purpose and before Product. Purpose should drive what you're ultimately solving for ... but do so in the confines of the profit necessary to be able to deliver on your purpose.

Looking back, I believe we could've done a better job of answering both our purpose and profitability in concert; were we starting over today, we'd take those both into account in that order. Purpose, then Profit, then Product.

The thought experiment we opened with in this section is one that scares a lot of people. Consider what happens to your business if sales and marketing are completely turned off.

If your answer to that hypothetical is that your business will go stagnant, you have some work to do on your product. If you're reading this and thinking, "Marketing and sales *are* my business!" that might be true today. But in order to hit a much bigger business goal, your targets have to shift. Marketing and sales are amplifiers, not essentials.

Top Problems in Product Creation

Relying on marketing and sales as the entire business isn't the only problem I see in working with companies trying to achieve their Billion Dollar Bullseye.

Here are the key areas to avoid if you want a product that will sell:

Don't under-research your market. Maybe you are your own best customer avatar. That still doesn't mean you can skip this step. You might be a naturally empathetic person, but that doesn't mean you understand the ins and outs of what your market is looking for. Put down the thought experiment of putting yourself in someone else's shoes and *go ask them what they want.*

(Bonus, this works for all relationships.) Give it a shot. It'll hands down produce your best results and best relationships—both personal and professional—but most importantly, it'll produce your best product.

Don't ignore customer feedback. Speaking of asking your customers what they want ... Ask and then stop talking. Don't analyze answers right away. Just listen. Don't ignore feedback because it bruises your ego or bristles your sensibilities.

I guarantee your product will easily hit the point of selling without marketing and sales—if you design a product your customers are asking for.

By the way, this is the area where I see nearly every business roll their eyes and say, "Oh yeah, we do that." What they mean is that they have a survey, or someone asking for feedback, but really, they're just looking at the feedback that validates their assumptions. For many, the hard or insulting feedback is an opportunity to argue with the customer, deride them as idiots, dilute their feedback as a small sample size, or use any other justification to avoid the implication that the product simply needs to be better.

Don't lose sight of the promise of your product. No one is going to care if your product has the coolest razor handle on the shelf if it can't provide a good shave.

Start big picture and then work your way down.

1. What is your product promising your customer?
2. What job is your product being hired to do, and what other hires can be made to do that job? [4]

---

4 Ulwick, Tony. "Jobs-to-Be-Done: A Framework for Customer Needs." Medium, January 6, 2017. https://jobs-to-be-done.com/jobs-to-be-done-a-framework-for-customer-needs-c883cbf61c90.

First and foremost, aim to capture that transformative customer experience. Afterward, supplement it with supporting details. Avoid getting overly absorbed in the specifics at the expense of your overarching promise.

Don't ignore market feedback. This is different from ignoring your customers. While it's true that you don't want a business that is too trendy, you need to know what your market's trends are and where your business fits. It does nobody any good to blindly stick to a product or a system because "This is how it's always been." Pay attention and shift as needed before your business becomes irrelevant to your customer base.

Don't skimp on product design. Chances are your customers won't sit through a series of 20-minute YouTube tutorials about your product— unless you're incredibly trusted and in a super niched-down world. Make your product as intuitive as possible for your user. Beta test. Keep the average customer in mind when designing and testing your product, and don't be afraid to reiterate your product if it's time. Designing, building, and testing your product is hard freaking work, but it's absolutely worth all of the points for this ring of the target. This has always been true, but in today's world with returns, chargebacks, and alternative purchases being effortless and prevalent, it's all the more important to have your product WOW at every possibility.

Don't take price for granted. We touched on this in the Profit ring. If you've priced your product too high, you've done your competitors a favor because your customer base will flock to them instead of you. If you've priced your product too low, you've also done your competitors a favor because your business won't be around for long. We'll talk more about pricing strategies later in this section, but remember that all business is an exchange of value.

My favorite illustration of this point is the urban legend around a very popular and elite Swiss watch brand. Don't worry, even if it's only a legend, it's still instructional. The story goes that they started selling watches, expensive, but not stratospherically expensive. But they weren't selling. Lo and behold, a reporter runs a story on the watches, a typo adds a zero to the price of the watch, and they're inundated with calls, resulting in a watch brand today that has timepieces selling for multiple millions.

So, what's the lesson here?

Price communicates value. Don't take price for granted. It's a strategic decision that determines where you show up in your market, how your customers expect to be served, and is of foundational importance to your Purpose, Profit, and Product.

Don't sell the same product as the next company. As Dan Kennedy said, "If you're in a commodity business, get out."[5] He didn't mean abandon your business; rather, differentiate it so you're not a commodity. It is essential to somehow differentiate your product from your competitors. Do not, I repeat, do not rely on marketing to make your product stand out. It's a trap. Every time. And it will sink your profit margins. Make your product different enough to stand out on its own. How? Circle back to the top of the list. Research your market and listen to your customers.

Do not rely on sales and marketing to save your product. We've talked about this, and it bears repeating: Be cautious of becoming a company that is super sales and marketing heavy. Be aware if you're looking to marketing because you're burned out on working on your product. I remember an early job I had just focused on getting more salespeople who were harder and harder closers. If you find yourself focusing on those areas without much consideration for your product, then all you're really doing is creating a surrogacy that'll vastly limit your overall success.

---

5   Kennedy, Dan. *No B.S. Sales Success in the New Economy.* Canada: Entrepreneur Press, 2010.

Creating a Transformational Product

Creating a transformational product seems like witchcraft. You need just the right mix of ingredients to brew the perfect concoction that'll launch your business forward. It's tedious work. But it's well worth your time, energy, effort, and money to make sure it is nailed on the head. Think of every investment in Product having multiplier effects for every area of your business. The better the product, the cheaper the marketing, the less of a burden on sales, etc.

Take Kajabi user Graham Cochrane for example. Graham started his first business in 2009 and, admittedly, had no idea what he was doing. He had a passion for music production and needed to make money. That's where Kajabi's purpose intersected with Graham's.

Since then, he's built two online businesses that now generate $160,000 a month in passive income, created in the five hours Graham invests *per week*. Prior to his experience using Kajabi, Graham had recently been laid off in the middle of a global recession. He even shared that his family qualified for government assistance in the form of food stamps (now called SNAPS). From government assistance to almost $2M in passive income?[6]

I'd call that transformational.

But, as you've seen, most business owners won't make the effort to make their product transformational. It's easier to throw together an average solution and get it out there than it is to think and do the real work. Most people take that shortcut because creating something that will transform lives is riddled with problems. You experience this every day, and so do I every time we search Amazon and get all the unbranded products from overseas that

---

6   Cochrane, Graham. "40-Year-Old Works 'Only 5 Hours a Week' and Makes $160,000/Month in Passive Income: 3 'Complete Lies' about Side Hustles." *CNBC Make It*, November 2023. https://www.cnbc.com/2023/11/02/40-year-old-works-5-hours-a-week-and-makes-160000-month-in-passive-income-dont-believe-these-side-hustle-myths.html.

we can't even pronounce the name of, yet we see 38 different "brands" for the same black headphones.

Here are a few of the bigger challenges to making a product transformational.

#1—The product is missing the "it will sell even if I don't market it" edge.

If the product is missing that inherent virality or transformational experience, it'll require tremendous marketing, sales, and other parlor tricks to sell it, resulting in terrible businesses and terrible margins because those types of companies and their owners are really just chasing money. They're not building actual value.

This is where the question, "If your business had no marketing, would the product grow on its own?" comes in. And if the answer is maybe, or the answer is no, then you probably don't have a great product, and you're probably not putting the energy into developing a great product.

From what I've seen, business owners often avoid focusing on improving their product. It's not sexy work. It's hard work.

The easy way is to ship your product and tell yourself it's just the first iteration and that you can improve on it later. But deep down, what you really mean is that you shipped a product that you don't actually want to deal with. Companies in this position keep going to sales and marketing as their fix because they already have the product.

We'll get into this later when we talk about teams, but nearly all people want to stay comfortable. That's true for your audience, and that's also true for the people you hire. They're not looking at how they can grow and stretch for the benefit of the customer. They'll look at their own benefit first.

Here's where I learned this lesson.

At Kajabi, two members of our C-suite really hated sales and marketing. When we asked them to add an important, customer-requested aspect to the product, they got squirrely.

"Ooh, I don't know. It feels so salesy. That's super aggressive."

I shot back only once that this ask would give our customers more options. Not everyone had to use the extra option, but we needed to give our customers the ability to choose.

But they won. They complained about it enough that Kenny and I threw our hands up and moved on.

Now, this is important: *I made a huge mistake in how I handled that interaction.*

In that moment, I let go of actually engaging in objective feedback about the product and its ability to deliver on its promise.

As such, whether I did it purposefully or not, I had put a greater burden on our customer experience team to be able to answer an objection that shouldn't exist.

I placed a greater burden on marketing to sell a product that didn't have a feature that its competitor did. I put greater pressure on sales initiatives to be able to move someone through the process without a crucial feature our product should have had.

I didn't ever think about it in those terms. To me, I was capitulating on a product feature, but what I didn't consider was *what that meant for everything else.*

What I should have said—and what you can say when you're faced with this dilemma—is:

"I understand where you're coming from. What you're really telling me is that I'm asking you to do something difficult. I'm asking you to do something out of your comfort zone. I'm asking you to do something that maybe your personal lens on life doesn't lend itself to doing, *but I need you to know that my job is to solve problems for our customers.*"

"If you're going to solve for your personal comfort or personal agenda over the success of our customers, I don't have a choice but to find someone that's going to solve for the success of our customers. I hope that that's you. But right now, what it sounds like is you're really arguing for your own comfort or your own limitations rather than telling me what you need to be able to move beyond that."

(Thankfully, Kajabi now has this feature and it's doing spectacularly well.)

That's a tough conversation and a hard line to toe. Boldness in advocating for your product and your customer base is what earns full marks in this ring of the target.

This is especially true when you are not the direct person to build your product.

Let's say you want to own a restaurant, but you're not a chef.

You better find a chef you trust who agrees with your purpose on why you want the restaurant to exist.

You don't have to be the chef. You don't have to create your own product. You just have to be willing to hire and hold expectations along the way.

If you let your chef dilute your expectations, you're going to lose. If you let your chef talk you out of the concept you want, you're going to lose.

The difference here is simple. Are you delegating or are you abdicating?

You can delegate to developers, even if you can't write code, but if you're abdicating to developers and you're unable to clearly communicate why an element of your product exists or what it should do, you're going to get hosed.

Hired team members will generally give you all of the reasons that are palatable to the outcome they want (which is to their benefit). And if you're naive enough to believe it without questioning it, the customer and company are going to suffer. You must effectively advocate for your product.

Remember the section in the first ring where we talked about push versus pull when sharing your purpose in public? If you're going to delegate to another professional, you better have a really clear purpose. And you have to find those people who agree with your purpose by pulling them in.

At the end of the day, your product excellence is on you, whether or not you were the one to actually create it. Pull team members who align with your purpose. Advocate unapologetically for your product and the elements that should be present.

#2—What if my product isn't going to create a transformational experience?

There are going to be limitations on the intuitiveness or impact of your product.

Maybe Tide detergent can't have a transformational experience. Maybe protein powder can't be a transformational experience. Maybe there are commoditized products that aren't transformational, but through the **strategy of Prestige**, they are able to create a transformational experience by looking at how the customer experience works and how the customer interacts with that brand and with that brand's community.

There are no shortcuts. It doesn't matter what the product is. There are ways to turn customers into fans and, ultimately, brand ambassadors.

When you think about it, it's all based on the human experience.

Provide amazing customer service: Make sure your customer service team is knowledgeable, responsive, and helpful. This can go a long way in making customers feel valued and cared for.

Create incredible products: Even if your product doesn't change lives, it should be high quality, reliable, and do what it is designed to do. This will help build trust with customers and keep them coming back.

Listen and listen more: Ask for feedback like you mean it. The good, bad, and downright ugly. It's the only way to level up your product so it meets and exceeds expectations.

In one of my earliest sales jobs, I took a call from a potential client who was very angry. Things got heated, we argued, and as you may expect, I did not get the sale. My boss came up to me later and said, "Jon, at some point in your career, you've got to decide: Would you rather be right, or would you rather be paid?"

I've always remembered what he said because, for me, I'd always rather get paid. I've taken that mindset into every job I've had since then, and I've tried to instill the same mindset into the customer service representatives I've trained throughout the years.

When someone is laying into you, taking out their bad day on you, complaining about features your product doesn't have that they wouldn't even be able to use yet if you *did* have them, pause before you match their anger with your own.

When they splash your Facebook group with their negativity or decide to post and tell the world what you're lacking, look for the validity in what they're saying. Look for their passion for what they do. Recognize that you have a product that people really care about—and you don't ever want to lose that fervor, even if it is being misconstrued or inappropriately applied in a particular interaction.

Ask, "Would I rather be right, or would I rather be paid?"

Authenticity culture: A key difference between commoditized brands is how the brand makes the consumer feel. Why would a customer choose your brand over another? It all comes down to the authentic culture within your business and the community you're creating.

Building a community: To give you an idea of what we're looking for within an authentic community, here are some of the community-building, product-enhancing, commodity-escaping activities Persil, a UK-based detergent brand, has carried out:[7]

"Dirt Is Good" campaign: In 2005, Persil launched its "Dirt Is Good" campaign, which aimed to challenge parents' perceptions of dirt and encourage kids to get outside and play. The campaign featured TV commercials, print ads, and online content, including a website where parents could share photos and stories of their kids getting dirty. Notice how this encouraged buyers to not only interact with the product but also gave them a platform to do what most people love best: brag about themselves and their families.

"The Amazing World of Clean" exhibition: In 2010, Persil created a pop-up exhibition in London called "The Amazing World of Clean." The exhibition featured interactive exhibits that explored the science of cleaning and the history of laundry. They even built a giant washing machine that visitors could walk through! Persil created a novel experience that needed zero buy-in from its community but drove engagement. It changed the way their customers experienced something as mundane as everyday laundry.

---

7   Campaign UK. "Persil Advertising, Marketing Campaigns and Videos." *Haymarket Media Group*, n.d. https://www.campaignlive.co.uk/the-work/advertiser/persil/7750.

"Clean Graffiti" advertising: In 2012, Persil used this technique to advertise its products in several cities around the world. "Clean Graffiti" uses a high-pressure water jet to clean a pattern or message onto a dirty pavement or wall. It's genius. The result is a temporary, environmentally friendly advertisement that fades away over time. Again, an out-of-the-box approach to create a novel experience that highlighted the key tenants that drove customers to buy Persil in the first place: cleanliness.

"The Science Museum Live" sponsorship: In 2011, Persil sponsored a series of live shows at the Science Museum in London. These shows explored the science of cleaning through experiments, demonstrations, and interactive exhibits. This pulled in more of a community feel (mostly local) and created yet another engaging experience for their target market: parents. They pulled in the clean angle and infused it with a dash of education—something this specific market highly values.

Customer retention is not just about the product itself but also about the experience of interacting with your brand. Get your market to engage beyond the normal ad. By focusing on providing a positive experience, you can build long-term relationships with customers, even if your product is not transformational.

This concept of community will show up in the subsequent rings of Prestige as well as in Promotion. Like all of the circles in the Billion Dollar Bullseye, one ring bleeds into the next, each added layer creating a powerful framework that will lead you to ultimate business success.

#3—Not enough people want what you do or make.

If you find yourself with a product or service that not enough people want (because it started out as a passion product and you perhaps didn't know or didn't want to know), then you've got to get real about what you really want and make some changes. You don't necessarily have to throw out everything you've done so far, but you do need to stand up and lead the charge.

Take Dollar Shave Club as an example. They entered a crowded and competitive industry dominated by big brands but found success by identifying a specific market segment that was not being adequately served—men who were looking for high-quality razors and other grooming products at a lower cost without going to the store.

Dollar Shave Club focused on providing these customers with a simple and convenient subscription service that delivered quality products straight to their doors. They differentiated themselves through irreverent marketing campaigns that resonated with their target audience and helped them stand out in the crowd. They spoke the market's language and were rewarded for it.

Through this strategy, Dollar Shave Club grew rapidly and was ultimately acquired by Unilever for $1B in 2016. Their success serves as a great example of the power of finding a niche market and focusing on providing exceptional value to customers.

Here is exactly what the Dollar Shave Club did:

They **reevaluated their target market** and narrowed their niche so they could easily target their ideal customers. Because of that targeted niche, they were able to focus their research to make sure their product met very specific needs.

They **refined their product** and told a story that captivated their audience. They **continued to create new products or services** specifically for that captive audience.

They went from selling razors and other shaving products to including toothpaste, body wash, deodorant, moisturizers, hair products, and other goods their growing fanbase loved. This diversification allowed Dollar Shave Club to attract new audiences, continue to increase their range, and by definition, increase their revenue.

This care and attention, combined with an easy sign-up on a user-friendly website, great social media across multiple platforms, and consistently excellent support, meant the Dollar Shave Club experience was second to none. They **built relationships** with their customers.

Using those relationships, they were able to build a strong **referral program** that rewarded customers for inviting their friends and families along for the ride.

With all that in place, it was easy for them to form **partnerships** with other organizations to expand their product range and reach new customers:

- **7-Eleven:** In 2018, Dollar Shave Club partnered up with 7-Eleven to offer its products in over 3,800 stores across the United States.
- **Lyft:** In 2019, they partnered with Lyft to provide free samples to passengers in certain cities.
- **The American Cancer Society:** In 2020, they partnered with the American Cancer Society to support the charity's "Real Men Wear Pink" campaign, raising funds for breast cancer research.
- **Fitness centers:** They buddied up with several fitness centers to reach gym goers. Example: luxury fitness club Equinox in 2016.

In the pursuit of business growth, maintaining flexibility is paramount. Stay open-minded and embrace experimentation to discover the strategies that resonate most effectively with your goals.

Create a Product with Inherent Virality and Flywheel Effects

A huge part of the long-standing, "Would your product sell without marketing or sales?" question is whether or not your product has inherent virality and flywheel effects.

Remember how Kajabi had a network effect so strong that, even after ads were shut down, we continued to grow at the same rate?

There are a number of ways to incorporate this "flywheel" effect into your business, and more specifically, your product design. In fact, you can look at our entire Bullseye Formula as one huge flywheel, constantly feeding off of itself to gain momentum and drive ongoing business growth and success.

This type of self-reinforcing system is a fascinating topic of study, but it doesn't have to be complicated to implement.

Consider user engagement. Are your customers using your product on a regular basis? If they're not, is there a system you could set up to encourage usage of your product? Social media can be a powerful tool for this sort of virality effect. Offer raffles for shares on Facebook. Create a point system for referrals. Encourage your users to engage with your product on a regular basis.

Design a network effect. Does your product increase in value as more people use it? Look at Kajabi. Their network effect was massive. Simply having industry icons use their platform to launch courses created a huge surge of users for Kajabi, who then leveraged that success into their very own Kajabi Hero program, essentially a network effect program.

Include a unique design or approach. This strategy can protect against competitors replicating your process. Take Kirby vacuums, for example. They have proprietary technology and patents that make their product inherently more useful in delivering a solution than any competitor. Exclusive partnerships also fit into this category. What can you do to differentiate your product in the market (while increasing its value to your market)?

Engineer positive feedback loops. Not every product will lend itself to this one, but if you can, do it! A great example is gamifying your course or app. The more your user interacts with your product, the more valuable it becomes to that person. Nothing creates self-sustaining momentum like a good ol' dopamine push.

Pay attention to market dynamics. I often hear companies start to buckle down when their market experiences a significant change. Resist the urge. Much like the advice to not panic when the stock market experiences a downturn (and that downturn subsequently creates the most wealth for those who know how to take advantage of the opportunity), the same goes for significant market changes. Pay attention and use these changes to your advantage. A shift in perception during a period of upheaval is all it takes to dethrone a market leader.

And if nothing else, make sure your product prompts a life-altering experience or has transformational value because people can't help but talk about it. I mentioned Kirby vacuums earlier. They only sell door-to-door ... but it's not with a sales pitch. They offer to vacuum something in their prospect's home. They let the product do all the talking, and even if you don't buy, they count on the fact that you'll tell your friends and family about the experience.

Creating a product that provides an experience people just can't help but share is a very high bar.

Make sure your product, at a bare minimum, is self-evidently delivering on the desire that is already within the marketplace. That is the very beginning of creating the self-sustaining momentum of a flywheel in your business.

Your Product and Customer Retention

Here's the question you need to pin on the wall: Is every customer in your business worth more to you the following year?

Whether or not you have recurring revenue (and you should try and find a way), you better be asking, "How am I going to get more from this customer base in the future?"

So, when you think about the problem you're going to solve or are currently solving, know that there are only three ways to grow a business:

1. Acquire more customers.
2. Sell your existing customers higher-priced items.
3. Sell to your existing customers more frequently.

You've got to make sure that you're asking how your business is building this into its DNA: Is every customer worth money next year?

Because, if at the start of every month, you're at zero and you have no certainty, no idea, and no plan to have your existing customers continue, you're going to be hurting.

This all comes down to Product.

If you have a mediocre product, then not only will people only buy once but they'll sure as hell make it difficult for you to sell anything to them again. On top of that, any customer success people you hire to support your mediocre product will have an impossible task, and you will end up with a disengaged and unhappy team.

So, what are you throwing a surrogate at when really you should be doing the work?

Are you the person who wants to buy $10K in Facebook advertising but doesn't actually want to split-test the headline? You're better off going to Vegas and betting on black ... at least it's a better story with better odds.

Take Aim ...

The foundation for scaling your business lies in crafting a successful product. It's no coincidence that Product stands as a fundamental component of the Billion Dollar Bullseye. Achieving substantial growth hinges on the ability of your product to effectively address market problems and fulfill critical needs.

A great product must be designed to offer value and meet a high demand.

This means you don't create a product you think might work (or that you're interested in or passionate about); you create one the marketplace demands. By focusing on creating products that offer value and meet a high demand, you increase your chance of creating a product that generates substantial profits.

However, creating a successful product might be the hardest thing you do. It requires market research, product development, tenacity, the occasional battle of wills, an annoying level of persistence, and sheer pigheadedness. If you want to create a great product, you need to adopt the "get rich slow" mindset, where the focus is on building a sustainable, scalable business rather than on making quick profits.

To do this, you will need to shift your mindset from being a consumer to being a producer. This means that you should focus on creating value for others rather than on consuming products and services. By adopting this mindset, you can identify gaps in the market and create products that solve problems or fulfill needs.

On top of all that joy, you need to consider scalability from the start. Not only must plenty of people want your solution but it must be easy to make and distribute in huge numbers. Hand-carved antique clocks are unlikely to turn into a billion-dollar business. Too slow. Too niche.

Time to See Where Your Dart Lands

1. What would happen to your business if you shut off sales and marketing? If your answer is "immediately collapse," then read this chapter again. Be honest and objective. Revisit your numbers.
2. Ask what your product really is. Be completely honest, raw, and transparent about your business. It will give you the insight you need to fix it.

_____

_____

_____

_____

_____

_____

_____

_____

_____

_____

Answer "YES" or "NO" to the following:

Statement	Yes	No
Your product solves a real problem people care about.		
People are ready to pay to have that problem solved.		
There is a natural and unforced scale of purchase that repeats year on year.		
Your product adds to your customers' lives to the degree that cost doesn't really matter to them.		
You stick to your guns when you're choosing between solving a customer problem or keeping your team comfortable.		
You have a test, review, and upgrade process in place that allows you to keep up with market trends and customer needs.		
You listen to your customers' questions, needs, whims, and desires and take their input seriously.		
You engaged with your customer base during development.		
If the team you have can't find or develop the best product, then can you find people who can? You don't compromise on quality and purpose.		

If you said "YES" to everything, then you've nailed Product!

If you have even one "NO" ... then do the work to turn that into a "YES."

How to Know You've Hit the Product Target

Hitting the Product target looks like momentum and enthusiasm that you couldn't stop even if you tried. You can't stop people from talking about it. You can't stop people from buying it. You can't stop people from referring their friends to it or posting about it online. That's the type of effect you want your product to have. You want your product to be so unique, so impactful, and so transformational that, through the delivery

Figure 6

The Expanded Bullseye: Purpose, Profit, and Product

of the product, people can't help but become part of the perpetual promotion machine that drives the success of the product.

Conversely, if you have a product that is easily forgotten, that is highly commoditized, that doesn't prompt referrals, love, or any interest, your market is going to be relegated to whoever is priced lowest, and you're not going to really nail Product. You're going to be dependent on the rings that follow this one, and it's going to be a constant cycle of finding the next campaign to hopefully stay ahead of having a product that doesn't market itself but requires marketing on marketing on marketing to succeed.

If the latter paragraph describes where you are, it's never too late to iterate your product or service. It will take work. It will take soliciting feedback. And it will take listening to that feedback. But with the right guidance, it can (and must) be done.

How Product Ties into the Rest of the Bullseye

If you have a great product, you're going to have a great team. If you have a great prestige strategy (see next chapter), you're going to have a great customer experience team.

Your team will only perform as bright as the stage they're on. Your job as the owner/entrepreneur is to build the best possible stage for your team by creating an incredible product. Another note that we'll touch on in the People section is that A-players only want to be on stages where they can shine brightly. The whole theory of "just hire talent and they'll fix everything" is true but flawed. No A-player is going to willingly jump onto a sinking ship and hope for the best.

Now, when you go outside of the core circles and move into Prestige, Promotion, Persuasion, and People, all of those things will only amplify your core three: Purpose, Profit, and Product.

If your company isn't running optimally and you've failed to nail Purpose, Profit, or Product, you're going to use the other rings as surrogates, compensating for your lack of foundational choices and actions in your business.

You'll end up supplementing a missed Product ring by overburdening the customer service team to answer all the questions that the product itself should answer.

You're going to need a proxy for Promotion, trying to market something that doesn't sell itself. Then, your Persuasion strategy quickly becomes hiring the hardest closers available.

Since all the other rings are failing, your only move for the People strategy will be trying to fill the constantly empty seats because no one cares enough about your Purpose to stay and see it through.

From Fundamentals to Amplifiers

When Kajabi began, we were a software as a service company, serving digital commerce entrepreneurs in an industry that was pretty nebulous and ready to be defined. Kajabi was (and still is) digital, and available immediately. We created the excitement of unboxing with pixels rather than the packages of physical CDs, pamphlets, DVDs, and the like that were popular in the industry at the time. And we were excited to see the business growing, but then the industry started to mature.

We started to see these trends defining "the creator economy." We started to see these trends of digital-first entrepreneurs that were creating brands around their knowledge, around their career proficiencies and experience, and all of a sudden, we asked ourselves, "Wait a second ... if this industry is growing at this level and rate of speed, there will eventually be a book written about it. And we're either going to be the subject of the book or we're going to be a footnote of the book. Which one do we want to be?"

If you've ever read *Play Bigger*[8] and the authors' work on category design, they talk about companies like Salesforce that own the category of software as a service. They talk about companies like Jabra that created three different categories yet own none of them. This is a key inflection point where you have to ask yourself if you feel confident enough in the fundamentals of your business, confident enough in the growth of the market that you'll dive headfirst into a season you've never experienced before.

You're going to dive into that experience with no end date and with very little certainty around what will be required.

It is at this point you have to know with certainty that you have nailed your three fundamental bullseye targets: Purpose, Profit, and Product.

---

8   Ramadan, et al., *Play Bigger*.

Without those, you are headed into space without a functioning rocket ship or knowing where you're going to land, but it's probably not where you're hoping to go. Without that core three, the following rings, the amplifiers, your growth, and success will be lackluster at best and constant sources of frustration at worst.

Before you continue, I strongly suggest you take a minute to review your core fundamentals, how you scored on your assessments, and what actions you need to take within your company before you move on to the four amplifier rings of the Bullseye Formula.

Chapter 5

Ring #4: Prestige

I've learned that people will forget what you said, people will forget what you did, but people will never forget how you made them feel.

—Maya Angelou

Let's continue to expand our bullseye to an amplifier that will assist you in achieving the promise of the Bullseye Formula.

A prestigious customer experience is critical, especially in the early stages of your business. And you're going to use this area of Prestige to supplement areas that will someday be product-led.

This sounds in direct conflict with the last section, but hang in there for a minute. Being product-led out of the gate is expensive, it's hard, it's elegant, and it can't be forced. Even limitless financing doesn't improve the odds of achieving it. *Product needs to be co-created with your user base.* The way to co-create with your users in the beginning, without sacrificing what the product needs to do, is with a prestigious customer experience.

During the time Kajabi was ramping up, other industry competitors were asking, "How can we do less? How can we serve less? How can we be less hassled?" Whereas at Kajabi, we kept asking the opposite, "How can we do more? How can we serve more? How can we show up where nobody else is?"

When other companies offered knowledge bases, Kajabi offered support tickets. When competitors caught on and offered support tickets, Kajabi offered live chat. When live chat became the norm, Kajabi upped their live chat to be available 24/7/365 and has since added dedicated customer success teams, a learning and development department, and industry experts to continue to expand prestige.

At every single level, Kajabi asked, "How can we make their choice of purchasing and partnering with Kajabi a prestigious experience, something that advances and broadens their status, their momentum, and their business?"

This was an amplifier that truly changed the game in an industry where Kajabi's success was based on the success of our users.

Without a prestigious customer experience for people to enjoy along the way, Kajabi would not have been able to continue iterating on the product and rounding out those rough edges that always exist in new products.

Now, Kajabi offers a free 30-minute call to anyone who signs up for our two-week trial. We don't outsource these calls, either. Each user is connected to one of our staff members. Oh, and this isn't a sales call. The goal is simple: Give each customer our full and undivided attention to learn how we can set them up to absolutely crush it with their business.

This level of prestige amplifies our external purpose (through supporting customer success), our profit (through increasing stick rates), and our product. (And customers have a better idea of the value stack within Kajabi when someone walks them through it and helps them see how the platform is designed with their goals in mind.)

Experience Customer Experience

The next step in your business is pretty simple: Experience what your customers experience. Have you actually walked through your own customer experience? Be honest, because no one does this.

I didn't do it nearly as often as I should've in my early days. But now, as a board member, investor, partner, or owner, I mystery shop often. Not because I uncover problems that are mine to own but because I now understand the value of experiencing the experience.

A company that shoots the lights out in the area of customer prestige is Disney. **They create and audit all of their experiences often, and it shows.**

Disney doesn't start at the ride. They don't even start at the line of a ride. They start all the way in the parking lot with the parking attendant. And they have been known to take it even further to sit down with the city boards in Anaheim and Orlando to design the road and traffic flow that goes into the park.

Once in the park, Disney is known for **personalizing the customer experience** by paying attention to every detail and creating a magical and memorable experience for their guests, from personalized greetings as they enter the park to customized birthday celebrations and personalized experiences at their hotels. When you visit Disney, it feels like the day was made for you.

They **tell stories** that resonate with customers on an emotional level and use those stories to create an immersive experience.

They **pay attention to every detail,** from the cleanliness of their parks to the way they interact with guests. Every aspect of the customer experience is crafted. Not just managed—but crafted.

They also **collect feedback and improve** ... and improve and improve. They don't quit.

When you implement this kind of customer retention philosophy, you will increase customer retention and create long-term relationships with your customers, which can lead to repeat business, positive reviews, referrals, and exponential growth.

Disney audits every single touchpoint (even the touchpoints you don't naturally think of). At every juncture, they ask, "Does this enhance the experience? Does this add more prestige? Or, is this a prestige-detracting element that we need to work on?"

You know what Disney is not doing?

Looking for the next ad agency to drum up sales. They're not hiring superstar salespeople or hunting for the next affiliate hack to get growth.

They drive through specifically designed traffic flows and audit every step of their park experience. From the parking pass you buy, to the shuttle you walk on, to the gate you walk through, to the first ride you go on, to the exit of the ride, to the first category of the gift shop, to the cafeteria line, to the napkin experience.

It is incredibly detailed, and Disney is always looking at *every single touchpoint.*

You may not offer something in person, but the principles remain the same. Have you audited and optimized every single touchpoint of your business? Are you looking at your retail distributors and testing the experience there?

Are you going through every part of your sales funnel online? Are you going through every element of your support experience and looking at how it actually impacts the customer? Or, are you just believing that if you throw your product to a big provider, or if you throw it to a retailer, that's going to provide a prestigious experience?

And the answer is it absolutely isn't.

How often are you revisiting it and improving it? Some people say, "I did it. I did it once. I'm done. I'm good." Unfortunately, once or even twice is not enough. Every single time you go through to optimize your customer experience, you're going to find more and more ways to enhance it.

Be honest with yourself.

- When was the last time you actually went through your own support process?
- When was the last time you went through your own sales process?
- When was the last time you went through your own marketing funnel?
- When you did, were you proud or so disappointed you never did it again?

The notion of customer prestige serves as a powerful amplifier ring on our bullseye, as the compounding benefits derived from prioritizing this aspect of your business are truly immeasurable.

Here are some companies (other than Disney) who've gotten this right:

Amazon. Known for customer obsession, Amazon has built its business around a convenient and seamless customer experience.

Zappos. Famous for its free shipping and returns, Zappos has a 24/7 call center and a 365-day return policy. This super generous customer service policy has skyrocketed its reputation above competitors.

Apple. You know the one. These guys have made the customer experience the core of their business (pun absolutely intended). From design detail to intuitive tech and generous returns with Apple Care to a personalized shopping experience. "Prestigious" is almost synonymous with "Apple" given their high levels of success in this area.

Nordstrom. A high-end department store, it's also known for exceptional customer service. The company has a reputation for going above and beyond to satisfy its customers, including offering free alterations and personal styling services. One time, they even accepted a return of four tires from a man who swore he bought them from Nordstrom. In reality, the man had bought the tires from a company that Nordstrom absorbed and rebranded, but the employee was still empowered to make it right.[1]

The Ritz-Carlton. Luxury in hotel rooms, dining, and service, the Ritz-Carlton has a set of service values known as the "Gold Standards," which not only guides every aspect of their customers' experiences but is also taught and duplicated across industries.

Southwest Airlines. Low fares, no frills, but plenty of great service. What makes it possible? The airline's employees are empowered to make decisions on the spot to improve customer experience.

Trader Joe's. Not many grocery stores can boast interesting and unique lines along with low prices. The appeal of Trader Joe's includes all that and a great customer experience—and that's not by accident. The company works on the philosophy that if they treat their employees well, their employees will treat their customers well, and it's paid off in hard cash.

In-N-Out Burger. A Southern California staple for the greatest burgers in the history of fast food. (Okay, I'm biased.) However, as a family-owned, values-driven business, their experience is top-notch in every category right down to not allowing DoorDash to deliver their food since they'd risk people having a poor experience.

Deliver a Prestigious Customer Experience in Your Business

What every company above (including Kajabi) did was create a completely differentiated and unique customer experience. This really comes from the adage,

1   Nordstrom. "The Nordy Pod: The Truth About Nordstrom's Legendary Tire Story." *Nordstrom Now* (blog). Nordstrom. August 1, 2022. https://press.nordstrom.com/news-releases/news-release-details/nordy-pod-truth-about-nordstroms-legendary-tire-story.

"People don't care how much you know until they know how much you care."

People aren't going to remember anything except the way you made them feel.

And this is another element of building that relationship with your customer. They're going to tell you how to develop a prestigious experience. Does it wow them? Is this something they've never experienced before? Are you thinking about what they need before they even say it? And, how are you wowing them in this process?

Books on customer care and service might tell you a whole lot about what specifically to do, but really, it boils down to this:

Listen, then do something about it.

When you listen, you develop an understanding of who specifically your customers are and what really matters to them. The more you know about what they need and want, what scares them, and what keeps them awake at night, the more able you'll be to add that goodness to your solution.

When you listen, you'll be able to respond quickly. People might have started the conversation feeling frustrated because something isn't what they expected, but when you listen, respond, and fix things, they feel heard and valued.

When you listen, you will find yourself able to provide a seamless experience. Start to finish. You can test the heck out of your product, but you know it. You know the quirks, the ins and outs of it. And you're forgiving of it all because you were there the day it was born. Your customers won't be. What is easy for you might not be for them. They'll tell you where the pinch points are.

When you listen, you'll learn what they like, don't like, want, don't want, and you'll know exactly what to offer them the next time they come in the door.

And because you're not the one sitting on the phone, you'd better train your team to listen.

Your team has to know every inch of the product. They have to know how to take crap from someone having a bad day. They have to be okay with conflict and be able to talk people down. Then, you have to give them the power to make things right.

Too many support desks work on scripts that get read verbatim. The person on the receiving end hears it, knows it, and is already writing a one-star review and tagging a hundred of their best friends.

So, it's simple. Listen.

Do you ask for feedback? Listen to it.

Then, add the magic and exceed expectations. Go above and beyond. Give your customers not only what they thought they needed, but dreamed they wanted.

By focusing on one core skill—listening—you will be able to deliver a world-class customer experience that will build your brand loyalty and drive business growth from where you are now to a billion-dollar business.

What Prevents You from Delivering a Prestigious Customer Experience?

Delivering the kind of customer experience that people talk about, share, and save up to experience time and time again (still have Disney on my mind) isn't easy. There are moving parts all over the place, and every one of those moving parts is human. We're designed to screw up, get emotional, take sides, and get annoyed. So, what gets in the way of you delivering an incredible customer experience?

#1 Problem: Not revisiting and improving customer experience on an ongoing basis

Not revisiting and improving customer experience on an ongoing basis is the best way to piss off your customer base. It can lead to a decline in the quality of service offered to customers. Customers' needs and preferences can change over time, so it's important to stay up to date with those changes and adjust their customer experience strategies accordingly. Failure to do so can result in a disconnect between the customer and the business. It's not hard to see that the disconnect leads to a negative experience that can tarnish your business's reputation and prevent repeat customers.

Failure to make improvements to customer experience leads to lagging behind competitors who are continually innovating and improving their customer service. In a competitive market, businesses need to stay ahead of the curve and offer something unique and valuable to customers. Consistently improving the customer experience is one way to differentiate your business from its competitors and create a competitive advantage.

Routine audits can help identify areas for improvement and inform the necessary adjustments to keep up with changing customer needs and preferences. By gathering feedback from customers, analyzing data, and regularly reviewing the customer experience, you ensure your business is meeting the needs of customers and providing a consistently exceptional experience.

#2 Problem: No differentiation

A lack of differentiation can make your company seem bland and tasteless, impacting a prestigious customer experience in several ways.

First, if your business is not able to differentiate itself from its competitors, it may struggle to attract customers who are looking for unique or innovative products or services. The market will go to the most obvious solution or worse—hop back and forth because they can't tell the difference between you and your competitor. As you can imagine, this makes it difficult for the company to build a loyal customer base and establish itself as a leader in its industry.

Second, a lack of differentiation can lead to a "keeping up with the Joneses" approach where the business simply tries to copy what its competitors are doing without adding any real value or innovation. This gives you a mediocre customer experience that fails to stand out in the marketplace.

Finally, if your company is unable to differentiate itself from its competitors, *it may have to compete primarily on price*, which can be a difficult and unsustainable strategy in the long term. In other words, a lack of prestige can make your profits suffer. Customers may be willing to pay a premium for a product or service that offers unique benefits or features, but they are unlikely to stick around if the only difference is a slightly lower price.

A fun differentiation example from Derek Sivers of CDBaby.com (sold for over $100M) is the thank you email after ordering a CD:

Your CD has been gently taken from our CD Baby shelves with sterilized, contamination-free gloves and placed onto a satin pillow.

A team of 50 employees inspected your CD and polished it to make sure it was in the best possible condition before mailing it.

Our packing specialist from Japan lit a candle and a hush fell over the crowd as he put your CD into the finest, gold-lined box that money can buy.

We all had a wonderful celebration afterwards and the whole party marched down the street to the post office where the entire town of Portland waved "Bon Voyage!" to your package, on its way to you, in our private CD Baby jet on this day, Friday, June 6th.

I hope you had a wonderful time shopping at CD Baby. We sure did. Your picture is on our wall as "Customer of the Year." We're all exhausted but can't wait for you to come back to CDBABY.COM![2]

Didn't require a ton of money. Just creativity. There's no reason to be boring.

•

#3 Problem: Inadequate communication

Customers want communication. Clearly, a communication breakdown can dismantle your prestigious customer experience in a number of ways.

First, customers may feel frustrated or confused if they don't receive clear and timely information about their order, account status, or other relevant issues. This can lead to a breakdown in trust and undermine the perception of the company as a prestigious brand.

Additionally, customers who have a difficult time communicating with a company may become frustrated and seek out alternative options, which can lead to lost business and a damaged reputation. These are not customers who are worth more the following year. This is especially true in today's digital age where customers expect to be able to quickly and easily communicate with companies through a variety of channels.

Make sure you have clear and open lines of communication with your customer base. This may involve providing multiple channels for customer communication, such as phone, email, and chat, as well as investing in tools and systems that can help streamline communication and make it more efficient. It may also involve training customer service representatives to be more responsive, empathetic, and effective communicators, as well as regularly reviewing and updating communication protocols and processes to ensure that they are working effectively.

---

2   Sivers, Derek. "The Most Successful Email I Ever Wrote." *Derek Sivers*, July 2011. https://sive.rs/cdbe.

I can't overemphasize this problem enough—and the real dollars it represents. The customer interaction may start with questions (even pre-sale questions) and then, as a result of the style, timeliness, or completeness of the communication, a routine question becomes a refund request. Don't let the revenue that you've worked hard to get in the front door run out the back door because of poor practices.

#4 Problem: Insufficient focus

If your business lacks focus, it may not be clear on its purpose. This makes everyone confused—employees and customers alike. When employees are not clear on what the company stands for, they may not be able to deliver a consistent customer experience. Additionally, when customers are not clear on what your company stands for, they may feel uncertain about doing business with you.

Insufficient focus can also lead to a lack of attention to important details that impact the customer experience. For example, a business that lacks focus may not be able to effectively manage customer inquiries or complaints. This can lead to frustrated customers who feel like their needs are not being addressed. Similarly, a business that lacks focus may not be able to effectively manage its product offerings, resulting in inconsistent or inadequate product quality.

To ensure a prestigious customer experience, it is important for businesses to maintain a clear focus on their core purpose. This includes providing employees with clear guidance on how to deliver an exceptional customer experience and investing in the resources necessary to manage customer inquiries and complaints effectively. By maintaining a clear focus on the customer and their needs, businesses can build a strong reputation for delivering a prestigious customer experience.

#5 Problem: Failure to establish thought leadership

When you fail to develop thought leadership, it can tear down the perception of your expertise and authority in your industry. Customers and potential clients may see the business as just another player in the market, lacking any unique insights or valuable knowledge. This can diminish the value that the business provides to its customers and the market, making it difficult to stand out and earn a prestigious reputation.

Additionally, without thought leadership, businesses struggle to communicate their value proposition effectively, which can make it difficult to attract and retain customers. Customers are more likely to choose businesses that have a clear and compelling vision, and that can offer valuable insights and expertise to help them achieve their goals. Remember sharing your purpose in public? In short, don't stop there.

To avoid this, businesses should invest in thought leadership through creating high-quality content, sharing their insights and expertise, and participating in industry events and forums. This will not only help to establish your credibility and authority, but it can also help build meaningful relationships with customers and other industry leaders. By doing so, your business can position itself as a trusted and respected authority in your field, which can lead to a prestigious customer experience.

#6 Problem: Inability to build relationships

When a business is unable to build relationships with its customers, it can lead to a lack of trust and a disconnect between the business and its customers. Customers feel as though they are just a number and that their needs and concerns are not being addressed. While this is how it feels when you look at numbers, you cannot give that impression in a customer care situation. Your customers will leave in droves and trash you in reviews.

Building relationships with customers requires effort and a commitment to providing value beyond the sale. This can be achieved through personalized communication, thoughtful follow-up, and a genuine interest in the customer's success. By taking the time to understand the customer's needs and concerns, your business can create a positive experience and build trust over time. This builds on itself, creating loyal customers that are worth more to your business and development with every passing year.

Failure to build relationships will limit opportunities for repeat business, referrals, and positive reviews. Customers are more likely to return to a business they feel connected to and recommend it to others. A lack of connection will lead to a loss of business and a tarnished reputation.

There's a reason a doctor's bedside manner is directly linked to the likelihood of a malpractice suit.[3] Studies show that a physician who spends time with their patients talking, listening, and even laughing with them significantly reduces their risk of being sued. Communication engenders connection, and connection builds trust, respect, and loyalty.

It's important for businesses to make relationship-building a priority and to continually invest in their customers. This can be achieved through ongoing communication, personalized experiences, and a focus on delivering value at every touchpoint.

Okay. That's enough of the bad news.

What do you do about it? How do you bring the right people together to create the kind of customer experience that'll expand your Billion Dollar Bullseye? How do you get your customer support, customer experience, customer success, and your community of users at large to bring this element of prestige to what you do?

---

3   Relias Media. "Physician Bedside Manner Linked to Malpractice Suit." *Relias Media*, May 1, 1997. https://www.reliasmedia.com/articles/48843-physician-bedside-manner-linked-to-malpractice-suit.

Routine Audits and Optimization of the Customer Experience

Keep it simple, but keep it personal.

Step one: You (or your team) do the following:

1. **Identify key touchpoints:** Determine the different touchpoints that customers have with your brand, including the website, customer service, product usage, and social media interactions.
2. **Set customer experience metrics:** Define metrics to measure customer experience, such as customer satisfaction scores (CSAT), net promoter scores (NPS), and customer effort scores (CES).
3. **Collect data:** Gather data from various sources, such as customer feedback, surveys, social media monitoring, and customer service interactions.
4. **Analyze data:** Use data analytics tools to identify patterns and trends in customer feedback, including common complaints, areas for improvement, and opportunities for innovation.
5. **Implement changes:** Based on the findings from the data analysis, implement changes to optimize customer experience, such as improving product quality, enhancing customer service, or creating personalized experiences.
6. **Monitor results:** Continuously track the impact of the changes on customer experience metrics and make adjustments as necessary.
7. **Repeat the process:** Regularly repeat the audit process to ensure ongoing optimization of the customer experience.

Step two: As I've mentioned, mystery shop.

Put on a wig and a purple hat (not required but recommended) and experience exactly what your clients and customers are experiencing. If you can't get away with it yourself, then send in an anonymous friend.

One More Thing ...

The more your clients love what you do, how you do it, and how incredible they feel every time they interact with you, the more your competition and your industry will hear about you too.

A prestigious customer experience enhances a company's reputation and increases customer loyalty.

When customers enjoy a positive experience with a brand, they tend to share that experience with others, ultimately resulting in heightened brand awareness and credibility—a phenomenon affectionately known as "word-of-mouth marketing." It's powerful! This, in turn, results in increased sales, higher customer retention rates, and a stronger market position.

And if that weren't enough to motivate you to nail the Prestige target in our Bullseye Formula, a prestigious customer experience can help to establish a company as a leader in its industry. By consistently providing an exceptional customer experience, a company can set itself apart from its competitors and position itself as the go-to resource for its customers.

On the other hand, if a company fails to deliver a great customer experience, it can negatively impact its prestige by damaging its reputation, eroding customer loyalty, and ultimately, leading to a decline in sales and market share.

Therefore, it's important for companies to prioritize customer experience and continually strive to improve it in order to maintain their preeminent position in the market.

Take Aim ...

Providing a prestigious experience is crucial for building a successful business. Whether you're just starting out or looking to take your business to the next level, customer service should be a top priority.

You have to go above and beyond. You have to enthrall and delight them, surprise them, and make them feel so loved that they look for every email you send because they know it's pure gold and will solve their problems.

You have to treat them with the respect and empathy they deserve.

Should you let them walk all over you and your team? No. You're free to fire a customer who is simply a bad apple. That's not only good business but good human practice. If you don't, then that small handful of people will take up a disproportionate amount of time, energy, and resources, and you won't ever make them happy. So ... love your clients and customers but also be willing to let them go, when necessary, too.

With that said, the prestigious experience your customers receive must include fast resolutions to any issue—questions answered, support delivered, drama-free services provided, problems solved, and promises kept. They must know that when they contact your team, they leave happy, supported, and even more in love with your service than ever. Because if people know that problems will be solved, they are forgiving when problems arise, no matter how big that problem is. If you leave them hanging, then the smallest problem will send them over the edge.

So, invest in your support team. Make sure they have everything they need to make problems go away. And if they can't, make sure they have a clear line of escalation to people who can.

Measure, test, and measure again. Identify the most common questions and complaints from your audience. Take proactive steps to address these issues, whether it involves fixing, building, creating, or inventing. Strive for comprehensive solutions, as offering only half of the solution may lead people to seek the missing piece elsewhere.

Time to See Where Your Dart Lands

DO THIS:

When you move into Prestige, you're going for the Disney effect. Use Disney as your measuring stick when you do the following:

1. Walk through your customer experience. Right now. If you absolutely cannot right now, put a non-negotiable time on your calendar when you can.
2. When did you last experience the full customer experience— good and bad—from the proverbial front gate to the trash cans out back?
3. What can you adjust, remove, or add to improve the prestige of your customer experience?
4. Now, put *another* date on your calendar for when you can walk through your customer experience again.

Think critically about your business, how you do things, and how your customers see and experience you.

Score zero for "not me" and five for "exactly me" or anything in between.

Statement	Score
You mystery shop in your business once a month.	
You audit your buying/engagement process regularly.	
You get customer feedback after every transaction as part of an automatic process.	
You gather customer feedback and actually do something with it!	
When people talk about what you do as an organization, they're right.	
Your customers talk you up on social media without any prompts from you.	
When people call your sales team, they're just looking for help, not to complain.	
When people call your support and ask the same questions, you fix it, so they never have to ask that question again.	
When you're choosing between your customers' experiences and your team's comfort, you always, 100%, focus on your customers.	

If you score below 20

Okay. You know what I'm going to say here. It's likely you're trashed or ignored on social media and review sites. If people buy from you once, they probably don't buy from you again. This is a tough place to build from because you're looking for new clients, new customers, and new income every day and every month. Relationships all need care, attention, quality input, and imagination. Above all, your customers need you to listen.

Hitting your Billion Dollar Bullseye will be just about impossible if you don't nail this ring. And the crazy thing is, of all the rings, this is one of the easiest ones to fix. People respond when they're listened to. They respond when they get the product and service they expect. People respond when their expectations are exceeded, and they definitely respond when they feel ripped off or conned.

So, LISTEN. Pay attention. Then, fix the things people complain about. Don't try to imagine what people need. Just ask them. They'll tell you.

If you score 21 to 35

Not bad, but you can do better. (I'm putting the stuff you should do in bullets so folks who scored less than 20 will do this too.)

- Take the time to really get to know your people and the experience they're having with your organization. Do it firsthand. Don't delegate this.
- Go online and order. Pretend you need help and phone for support.

- Return the product and see how easy or difficult it is.
- Go online and complain to see how fast someone steps up to help you.
- Engage with every aspect and element of your business, and ask if you, as a customer, feel good enough to rave about your company. If not, fix it.

If you score 36 to 45

On one hand, I want to say brilliant, well done, or you've nailed this. On the other hand, I want to look you in the eye and ask if you've been honest with yourself.

Either way, do what I've suggested people who scored in the low and mid-range do. Disney doesn't sit back just because they've got it right. They keep searching for ways to be better because there's one thing you can be sure of: If you're getting rave reviews for doing something incredible, it won't be long before your competitors do the same, and you have to do something else to stand head and shoulders above the rest.

This isn't an area you can do once, decide you've cracked it, and never look at it again. This is a moving target and is the most public if you get it wrong. Remember, no matter your industry or product, it costs multiples more to acquire a new customer than to keep or sell more to an existing one ... don't miss the opportunity.

How to Know You've Hit the Prestige Target

Hitting your target in the Prestige category means receiving reviews and comments that indicate surprise and delight from customers. The objective is to craft an experience with touchpoints that are exceptionally enjoyable and effortless, surpassing the expectations set by other providers. The ultimate goal is to astonish customers with the speed, ease, and impact of the resolutions provided.

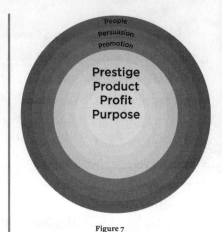

Figure 7

The Expanded Bullseye: Purpose through Prestige

It is crucial to identify minute differentiators that create a profound outcome. Even a marginal 5% improvement over competitors can become a remarkable strategic advantage, setting in motion a flywheel effect where customers eagerly spread positive word-of-mouth reviews and develop a strong desire to continually engage with and use your product. It's the fusion of these small, powerful differentiators that will propel your business forward. By embodying a mindset of continuous improvement, even the slightest edge over the competition can yield substantial results.

By consistently exceeding customer expectations, you cultivate a reputation for unparalleled service that breeds customer loyalty and advocacy. The key lies in going above and beyond, ensuring that every interaction leaves customers pleasantly surprised. Strive to create a customer journey that stands out from the crowd, evoking positive emotion.

Prestige is one of the targets of the Billion Dollar Bullseye that allows you to dream without spending dollars. You can create an incredibly prestigious experience for your customers without spending a penny just by separating yourself from the pack. What does that look like for you? It largely depends on your audience and product, but I promise you it *can* be done.

How Prestige Ties into Promotion

Every ring is impacted by the one before and after it. Prestige supports Product because no matter how hard you work, elements of a product may not be intuitive, may not be self-evident, or may not be product-led. Even if you think your product is simple or your instructions could be understood by a three-year-old, there will be people who disagree. And if you don't give them a great experience as they work things out, they'll be vocal in their displeasure. If you give them the red-carpet treatment, no matter how dumb you think they've been, they could become your biggest, loudest advocates.

Looking forward, Prestige naturally ties into Promotion by virtue of the fact that if your existing clients and customers rave about you, new clients and customers are going to be easy to persuade.

It's a no-brainer.

So, let's take a look at Promotion.

Chapter ❻

Ring #5: Promotion

The aim of marketing is to know and understand the customer so well, the product and services fit him and sells themselves.

—Peter Drucker

We're now onto our second amplifier, Promotion. My goal here is to completely reorient your thinking about marketing.

To be clear, **Promotion refers only to the world of marketing—not sales.** It's where you promote the promise of what you offer.

What is the promise of your business and how well is it being promoted?

Elon Musk discusses brand as simply customer perception, and that the perception will match reality over time. Meaning, if you promote consistently enough, the world can't help but catch up with how your promotion and marketing are positioning your brand.

At Kajabi, we learned the amplifying nature of promotion once we understood what truly drove results in our business. We had tried multiple times to perfect the paid media scaling. We tried to perfect the sales process, but it wasn't until we unlocked two core areas that we watched promotion completely take off.

Those two areas?

Recognition and referral.

In my time with Kajabi, we created the Kajabi Hero program (hat tip to Kenny, as he named it). This program was designed to give people an opportunity to feel involved in something bigger than themselves. Online entrepreneurship can be very lonely. You're stuck in front of a screen all day, and you spend a tremendous amount of time telling your family that you're actually doing something only to hear back, "Whatever. Nobody makes money online. It's a scam."

It's definitely a weird, weird world. And we showed up for these online entrepreneurs in a simple way: rewards. Every time they experienced some revenue goal in their business, we sent them something in the mail and asked them to post about it. The original gift was just a T-shirt.

It has now moved into a multifaceted, multitiered recognition program that follows people all the way to seven figures in their business and beyond. It even comes with different bespoke online communities of others who have also gotten to that level of success. It also now has a fully customized shipping box experience that opens up and creates a whole bunch of theater. It's super fun.

Eventually, our Hero program moved into our perpetual promotion machine where, whenever we recognize somebody with a growing business, it ties back into the network effects created in Product. After that person is recognized, we encourage them to join our partner program. Essentially, the message is, "Congratulations! You're experiencing success. You're teaching people all over the world via this platform. I bet all the people who are being taught through this platform would probably love to know what platform you use. Why don't you use this affiliate link? And we'd love to also send you some money."

We watched this flywheel go faster and faster and faster. The more partners we got, the more heroes we created. The more heroes we created, the more partners we got. And it has continued to today, as I write this book. It is still the most effective, organic channel Kajabi has, and it all stems from Napoleon Bonaparte. He said, "A soldier will fight long and hard for a bit of colored ribbon."[1] A bit morbid, but it serves to drive the point home. Recognition is everything for all of us.

Here's how Promotion amplifies the three core rings of Kajabi's Bullseye Formula:

- **Purpose:** Experiencing success alone and uncelebrated is not nearly as powerful as being celebrated for your accomplishments. The Kajabi Hero program positioned us as partners in their success, motivating our customers to achieve more, and hitting on our external purpose.
- **Profit:** Our affiliate program became another growth strategy for both us and our customers. Mutually beneficial, every month, an affiliate partner gets paid for anyone who has purchased Kajabi through them. This goes on in perpetuity. By sharing what they've built through Kajabi organically, we earn a new customer, and our users receive additional income from the 30% commission we pay our partners for the life of the new account.
- **Product:** Our affiliate programs showcase our product, its features, and its benefits better than any ads or marketing we could possibly create on our own.

If you're not incorporating recognition with your referral strategies and, ultimately, revenue, I'm telling you, you're missing out. If you're not incorporating recognition within your employee culture, you're missing out. I cannot overstate what this amplifier will unlock for your business.

There's another quote from a copywriting legend that I believe in so strongly that it informs my whole promotion strategy for whatever company I'm working with. It's by Eugene Schwartz from his book *Breakthrough Advertising*, and it says:

---

1   BrainyQuotes. "Napoleon Bonaparte Quotes." *BrainyMedia Inc*, 2024. https://www.brainyquote.com/quotes/napoleon_bonaparte_108401.

"Let's get to the heart of the matter. The power, the force, the over-whelming urge to own that makes advertising work, comes from the market itself, and not the copy. Copy cannot create desire for a product. It can only take the hopes, dreams, fears, and desires that already exist in the hearts of millions of people and focus those already existing desires on a particular product. This is the copywriter's task: not to create this mass desire, but to channel it, to direct it. Actually, it would be impossible for any one advertiser to spend enough money to actually create this mass desire. He can only exploit it. And he dies when he tries to run against it."[2]

So, how well do you know the hopes, dreams, fears, and desires of your market? How well is your marketing speaking to them? Are you using them as a litmus test for every piece of marketing and communication before it ever sees the public? My guess is not, as nearly all businesses simply resort to discounts or me-too style promotions that they see elsewhere.

In my own life and experiences, I realized that if my product wasn't doing exactly what I wanted it to, I would just try a better campaign. Promotion was my addiction. That's where I would always go to supplement or surrogate problem areas in my business. If the product feature I wanted wasn't out yet, I'd find some other source of sizzle or excitement to highlight and hype.

And this is the area that I see almost every business owner focus on to the detriment of their business. The belief here is, "If I just had the right marketing guy …" or, "If I just got a better agency …" or, "If I just fixed my onboarding or acquisition strategy …"

But what they're all really saying is, "My product is bad and I'm sad about it, but I don't want to look at it or improve it."

---

2   Schwartz, Eugene M. *Breakthrough Advertising*. Bottom Line Books, 2004.

So, you keep going down this rabbit hole, wondering how to do this whole marketing thing better. The reality is that you can polish a turd, but it's still a turd.

This is such a crucial area that so many people get so lost in. They misallocate resources, team efforts, and intelligence because they are unaware of what they're really avoiding by needlessly focusing on promotion.

Let's take a look at a few companies that get the Promotion target right:

1. From its iconic Christmas ads to its personalized "Share a Coke" campaign, **Coca-Cola** has mastered the art of emotional connection with its customers.
2. When it comes to storytelling, few do it better than **Nike**. Their "Just Do It" campaign, and everything that goes with it, has turned them into one of the most recognizable and successful brands in history.
3. Sleek and stylish, **Apple** appeals to the artist and maverick, and their "Think Different" campaign turned technology (great as it is) into a symbol of creative inspiration. They use that to set themselves apart from Microsoft, which comes across as all-business and stuffy by comparison.
4. The hilarious and irreverent "The Man Your Man Could Smell Like" campaign gave **Old Spice** a viral sensation, effectively reaching a whole new generation of buyers. Not a lot of companies that started in 1937 can claim that victory.
5. Say "gives you wings" to anyone and **Red Bull** will almost certainly come to mind. For these guys, it's not just the slogan and the ads. It's a daredevil, action-driven tribe they've built around them. Nobody wants to sleep on Red Bull's watch.

If you look at the big picture, all of these companies follow the same principles:

1. **Clear value proposition:** Companies with great promotions clearly communicate the value of their products or services to their target audience. They focus on the benefits that their customers will receive from using their products or services.

135

2. **Personalization:** Companies with great promotions tailor their messages and offers to the specific needs and interests of their target audience. They use data and insights to understand their customers' preferences and behaviors, and they use this information to create personalized experiences that resonate with their audience.

3. **Emotional appeal:** Companies with great promotions know that people make decisions based on emotion. They use storytelling, humor, and other emotional appeals to create a connection with their audience and make their brand memorable.

4. **Omnichannel approach:** Companies with great promotions use a variety of channels to reach their target audience. They leverage social media, email marketing, content marketing, influencer marketing, and other channels to create a cohesive and integrated campaign that reaches their audience where they are.

5. **Incentives and promotions:** Companies with great promotions offer incentives and promotions to encourage their audience to take action. They use limited-time offers, discounts, and other drivers to create a sense of urgency and motivate their audience to make a purchase or take another desired action.

These are just a few examples of tactics that companies with great promotions use. The key is to create a comprehensive strategy that combines these tactics in a way that is tailored to your target audience and supports your overall business goals.

This is great, good, and important, but out of every tactic, strategy, and tool a company uses, emotion is the one that outweighs the others a billion to one when it comes to connecting with a target audience.

You'll notice none of these companies do anything by accident:

Happiness. Joy. Togetherness. **Coca-Cola** has long been associated with positive emotions and memorable experiences. Their promotions focus on sharing moments of happiness and connection. They've taken personalizing bottles and cans beyond names to a whole label design that you can do directly from their website.

Inspiration. Athleticism. Dedication and hard work to overcome challenges. **Nike** feeds on people's ambitions and drive to succeed. The tagline "Just Do It" embodies the company and has become a mantra for its fans.

Exclusive. Innovative. A desire for simplicity and style. **Apple** taps into the human desire to be in the "cool kids" club by using cutting-edge products with a clean and minimalistic design.

Humor and an almost silly self-confidence. **Old Spice** is famous for not taking themselves too seriously. They use comedy and hyperbole to position their brand as a way for men to feel confident and attractive to others.

Adventure. Excitement. Fearlessness. If you're planning a weekend of wild rides, insane stunts, late nights, thrill-seeking, or high-energy madness, then it goes without saying that you and your adrenaline-junkie friends will be packing **Red Bull** like your great-grandad used to pack whiskey. Red Bull positions itself as a brand that can help its fans break through barriers and achieve goals, no matter how ambitious or difficult they seem.

You'll also notice none of this is easy! Mistakes are made and learned from. Learn from my mistakes and avoid the following.

Top Mistakes Companies Make When It Comes to Promotion

#1 Mistake: Acquiring customers at a loss with no idea how to recapture the loss and turn it into profit

Acquiring customers at a loss without a plan for recapturing that loss and turning it into a profit can be a risky strategy. In the short term, it may help to grow the customer base, but it can ultimately lead to financial difficulties and business failure. Everyone remembers the joke, "Bill, we're taking a lot of losses on this campaign." "Jim, you idiot, we'll make it up in volume."

If a company is consistently acquiring customers at a loss, it means that the cost of acquiring each customer is higher than the profit it generates. This leads to a situation where the company is losing money on each customer they acquire, and if they are unable to turn those customers into profitable ones, the losses can add up quickly and spit you right back out in the gutter.

This can feel like the right thing to do until the money runs out and you're forced to shut up shop or rely on external financing to stay afloat, which is expensive and difficult to secure when your numbers don't stack up. If your losses continue to accumulate, you'll have reduced investment in other areas of the business like Product and Prestige, which will continue to damage the company's long-term prospects and definitely kill any chance of turning what you have into a highly scalable business.

In short, acquiring customers at a loss without a plan for recapturing that loss and turning it into a profit is risky and unsustainable.

It is imperative to possess a clear comprehension of your customer acquisition costs and concentrate on strategies that maximize their lifetime value.

#2 Mistake: Lack of target

One of the biggest mistakes companies make with their promotions is failing to target their audience effectively. They might use generic messaging or promotional tactics that don't resonate with the specific needs, wants, or interests of their target market. This can result in low engagement, poor conversion rates, and wasted resources.

For example, if a company is promoting a product or service that is targeted at a specific age group or demographic, but its promotional efforts are too broad and don't speak directly to that group, it may miss the mark and fail to generate the desired interest or engagement.

Similarly, if a company tries to appeal to too many different groups or demographics with a single promotional campaign, it may dilute its message and fail to make a strong impact on any of the groups they are trying to reach. This leads to a lack of interest, engagement, and, ultimately, a lack of sales or revenue.

When this happens, the real target market is unforgiving.

In 2017, Pepsi released an ad featuring Kendall Jenner that depicted a protest march where the participants were seen holding up signs with vague messages such as "Join the conversation." The ad was widely criticized for trivializing and co-opting social justice movements for commercial purposes. Many felt that the ad was targeted at a younger audience and failed to resonate with them due to its lack of authenticity and insensitivity toward the issue at hand.

In the late 1990s, McDonald's launched a new burger called the Arch Deluxe, which was positioned as a more sophisticated and upscale product targeted toward adults. However, the campaign failed to generate enough interest among the target audience who perceived McDonald's as a fast-food joint for kids and families. The product was eventually discontinued, and McDonald's took a financial hit due to the unsuccessful campaign.

In both of these examples, the promotions failed because the companies failed to accurately target the right audience with their messaging and positioning. This highlights the importance of understanding the audience and tailoring promotions to their specific needs and preferences.

#3 Mistake: Focus too much on the product instead of the solution

Another mistake is focusing on your precious product instead of the problem it solves.

Take Microsoft Zune for example.

The Zune was released in 2006 as a music player to compete with Apple's iPod. Microsoft focused on the Zune's technical features, such as its large screen and wireless syncing capabilities, rather than highlighting the benefits that would appeal to consumers.

As a result, the Zune failed to gain traction in the market despite heavy promotion and marketing efforts. Consumers were not convinced that the technical features of the Zune were enough to make it a better choice than the iPod, which had a better user experience and a more intuitive interface.

The failure of the Zune underscores the importance of highlighting the benefits of a product or service rather than just focusing on its technical features. Consumers want to know how a product will solve their problems and make their lives better, not just what technical specifications it has. It's the difference between saying 16 gigabytes of storage versus Steve Jobs's infamous "1,000 songs in your pocket."

#4 Mistake: Your promotion isn't omnichannel

When a message isn't being delivered consistently across all channels where the target audience is present, it can lead to missed opportunities to engage with potential customers and convert them into loyal ones.

For example, if a company runs a promotional campaign only on social media but not on email, it may miss out on potential customers who are more likely to engage with email promotions. Or, if a company runs a promotional campaign only on TV but not on social media or email, it may miss out on potential customers who don't watch TV but are active on social media or check their email regularly.

In essence, not having an omnichannel promotion strategy can limit a company's reach, limit customer engagement, and hinder the success of the promotion.

Remember all the failed companies we discussed in Profit? All struck out when it came to being omnichannel.

#5 Mistake: Not knowing the difference between free swag and earned rewards

Swag is great and most people love it. They don't love junk, so think before you spend on stuff that lands in the trash two doors down.

However, even amazing swag can be seen as junk if it's just a giveaway. Remember, SWAG is the acronym for "stuff we all get," and it started with all the free stuff given away at trade shows.

Giveaway swag is expensive and may serve a purpose, but it's not always the best use of your money.

For example, typical swag is the stuff Red Bull gives away. They frequently give out free samples of their energy drink as well as promotional items, such as T-shirts, hats, and stickers. This has helped to build a loyal fan base and create a strong brand identity.

Dropbox took a slightly different route in its "space race" promotion. In this promotion, Dropbox offered free extra storage space to colleges and universities that signed up for the service. The more students that signed up, the more storage space the school received. This incentivized students to use the service and also helped to spread awareness of Dropbox to a wider audience.

Then there's Tito's Handmade Vodka, which has become known for its cute and clever swag items, such as dog bandanas, hats, and coasters. This has helped to build a loyal fan base and create a strong brand identity, as well as promote word-of-mouth marketing.

Google is known for its swag, which includes everything from T-shirts and socks to high-end electronics. Apple is another company that is famous for its swag, including branded accessories like hats and backpacks. Other companies known for their swag include Microsoft, Facebook, and Amazon.

Gucci, on the other hand, is known for giving out exclusive swag to its customers. Some examples of Gucci swag that the company has given out in the past include limited edition items, such as bags, keychains, and other accessories that are made from high-quality materials and feature the brand's signature designs. These items are often given out to customers who make large purchases or to VIPs who attend Gucci events or shows. The cost of these items can vary depending on the specific item and the materials used, but they can be quite expensive due to their exclusivity and the prestige associated with the Gucci brand.

All this adds up to a huge "So what?" It's free stuff for doing nothing other than showing up. You'll also notice that these strategies weren't employed until the company had more than enough money and a large enough brand for it to be helpful.

Here's something you need to get.

Marketing is often an area where it's easy to stay busy without achieving meaningful results. If you hand out a million T-shirts, that's great! But did anything come of it? Did the right audience even get them? Are they stuffed behind a wardrobe? Or have they been turned into a dog's chew toy? These are questions you have to ask and be honest about. This is the mistake companies make when it comes to giveaways.

Because there's a difference between free swag and earned rewards. Not only for your customers, but for you.

One Quick Way to Improve Promotion

I'm a 42-year-old dad with a body built by In-N-Out Burger. If you're a personal trainer and you're trying to sell me on a training program, you might start by asking, "What are some of your goals?"

I'd respond by saying, "I want to lose weight and be healthier."

Here's where most of us fall short. We stop asking questions and we start selling. Instead, take this opportunity to dig in and discover your customer's *actual* why—the benefit of the benefit.

There's a deeper, underlying "why" that's driving the decision-making process. Your customer may not even be aware of their own thinking. They may not have even verbalized it to themselves. Instead of identifying the immediate benefit, continue your exploration through questions and listening.

I recommend at least three "levels" of why. To use my earlier example:

Trainer: "What are your goals?"

Me: "I want to lose weight and be healthier."

Trainer: "How would your life change if you lost weight and got healthier?"

Me: "I'd have more confidence and more energy."

Trainer: "What would more confidence and energy result in?"

Me: "I'd be a good role model for my daughter and more active as she grows older."

Ahhh. Did you see that? The benefit of the benefit.

Your entire sales strategy has shifted because you're no longer selling numbers on a scale. You're selling legacy, and you're selling more and better time spent with loved ones. The #1 question every customer is asking is, "Can you get me from my current state to my desired state with as little stress and friction as possible?"

The questions you ask are to understand:

1. What is their desired state?
2. What emotions are driving that desire?

To summarize:

- Don't start selling too soon.
- Go at least three levels deep.
- Identify the benefit of the benefit.
- Align your offer accordingly.

Take Aim ...

You have to know your audience. The number of businesses that try to promote a product without a full understanding of their target market astounds me.

Take the failure of the Ford Edsel in the 1950s. The Edsel was intended to be a high-end car that would compete with luxury brands such as Cadillac and Buick. However, Ford made a number of missteps in their product promotion efforts that ultimately led to the car's failure, including not fully understanding their target market.

They believed that there was a market for a high-end car that would appeal to young families and upwardly mobile professionals. However, they failed to conduct adequate research to validate this assumption. As a result, the Edsel was designed with a number of features that did not resonate with their audience, such as a vertical grille that was widely criticized for its odd appearance.

In addition, Ford spent an enormous amount of money on a flashy marketing campaign that was widely criticized for being over-the-top and out of touch with the values of their target market. They also failed to adequately train their salespeople, who were unable to effectively communicate the benefits of the Edsel to potential buyers.

As a result of these missteps, the Edsel was a commercial failure. Ford lost an estimated $250 million (equivalent to over $2B today) on the project, and the brand was ultimately discontinued in 1960.

Beyond understanding the audience, you and your team have to have a deepening and enduring understanding of the product and everything it can do. Not only is this obviously essential when it comes to Promotion, but it helps you stand out in a crowded market. And not just stand out once but over and over again because Promotion isn't a one-time thing. It requires an ongoing effort to build brand awareness, generate leads, and drive sales. This is an all-in affair that has to be sustained, measured, assessed, upgraded, uplifted, and repeated over time.

And I don't say "measured" lightly. Your promotion has to be data-informed. No exceptions. Know your numbers. We talked about this in Profit. If you don't know your numbers, your business is built on quicksand. And I say data-informed as in—it's fine to test things that you may not be able to measure (i.e., media that is difficult to track), but if you're not seeing it move some needles, it's likely a waste of time.

Finally, Promotion is a team effort. It's not something your marketing team does on their own. It takes input from designers, the product team, the support team, finance, and the leaders ... Everyone has a different view, different experience, and different insights they can offer. Where companies fail is by making the "marketing department" responsible for all promotion, then sacking them if it doesn't work when, actually, you have a bad product, and guess what, the janitor could have told you that.

Time to See Where Your Dart Lands

1. Check out your competitors. What are they doing? Look at their Facebook Ad Library. Study their ads. See how long they've been running them. If they've been running the same ads for years, they probably work!
2. Assess the stuff you give away and why. If you don't give away anything, how can you start and start strategically?
3. Take a moment to consider your team. Do they know you've got their back? That they're part of a great solution? Do they care?

_____

_____

_____

_____

_____

_____

_____

_____

Okay. It's time to think again. This one's easy.
Answer "YES" or "NO" to the following questions:

If you were a stranger to your business but you were also the ideal customer...	Yes or No
Would the ads get your attention?	
Would you engage with your product or service beyond the basics?	
Would you ignore incentives as a cheap trick to get you to spend more, or would you see them as a way to get the most out of the product?	
Would you be willing to work for the prize at the end of the drive, or is it not worth the effort?	
Would you talk about the product or service? Would you rave about it?	
Would you give them a video testimonial if they asked you for one?	

Yes or no?

If "YES," then keep doing what you're doing, and do it better.

If "NO," then get this ring right because it has
a massive impact on the next circle.

How to Know You've Hit the Promotion Target

Now added to the growing bullseye, Promotion is supported by Prestige. As you'll see, if you have poor systems starting at the center and moving outward, each successive ring now requires a lot more work and a lot more effort.

People
persuasion

Promotion
Prestige
Product
Profit
Purpose

Figure 8
The Expanded Bullseye: Purpose through Promotion

So, if you've screwed up in Purpose, Profit, Product, or Prestige, Promotion is now going to have a much higher customer acquisition cost (CAC). It's going to have a much heavier burden of reinvention and message to combat market fatigue. You're going to ask for more from your marketing than you ever have because all of the other categories are not doing what they need to do, and that gets to be very problematic.

But, if you're nailing each of those rings in order, you see the exponential value increase as you continue throughout. It's going to frame a lot of that prestigious experience because Promotion is the first part of Prestige. It's Promotion that's going to frame how Prestige happens, how Product is viewed, how Profit is earned, and how Purpose is shown.

Hitting the Promotion target means that you have campaigns that are so enjoyable that people are seeing value before they ever purchase your product. That value could be feeling entertained, that value could be feeling educated, or that value could be feeling motivated and enthusiastic to take the next step. Promoting well means you are already delivering value, even before you actively start selling.

Hitting the Promotion target means you have entered a conversation going on in your customer's mind. You've spoken to their pain points so well that they're wondering if you know them better than they know themselves. You've made them believe that you have been where they are, and you can take them where they want to go. You have positioned yourself as their hero.

Promotion is the creation of knowing, liking, trusting, and getting a customer emotionally committed enough to take action.

Numerous books delve into the realm of marketing, yet it's essential to recognize that a one-size-fits-all approach won't suffice without a deep understanding of your Purpose, Product, and audience. I strongly advise against adopting indiscriminate marketing tactics, as they could potentially harm your credibility and hinder your capacity for substantial scaling.

How Promotion Ties into Persuasion

There's a reason Promotion comes before Persuasion in the framework. The more aware your ideal customers are of your business, the easier it'll be to get them on board.

Promotion is more than just bling, lights, and free stuff. It's about education. The more educated people are about what you do, how you do it, and how you can solve their problems, the more likely they are to jump in.

By effectively promoting your business, you can influence the perceptions and attitudes of your target audience, creating a positive image and building trust and credibility.

These two rings are naturally linked. Your Promotion is already a form of Persuasion. Your ad copy has to be persuasive. Everything you do has to entertain, educate, inform, and, ultimately, persuade.

It's all about showing people that you have a solution that works for them. When they believe you, they go from passersby to curious, to interested, to customers, to fans.

There are a lot of exits off that journey road. Persuasion keeps them on track.

So ... on that note, let's take a look at Persuasion in the context of hitting your Billion Dollar Bullseye.

Chapter 7

Ring #6: Persuasion

Escape competition through authenticity.

—Naval Ravikant

You've likely guessed it: Persuasion is the way you talk about sales.

Sales is often confused with the world of marketing. And the people who blur that line the most are the actual marketers and salespeople because they generally want the fault to be someone else's. Marketing always provides perfect leads but it's not working because the salespeople suck. And salespeople can't sell because the leads marketing provides are garbage, and around and around it goes. But that won't be the case for you because, arriving here, you already nailed Promotion.

Persuasion is a powerful amplifier to the core of your business, and it's meant to pick up where Promotion needs to leave off. Persuasion is not meant to do the job of Promotion and vice versa.

Some businesses have marketing and sales built as a synonymous department, and we'll talk about that in a bit. Even if that is your business, you must understand the clarity of those two roles. More specifically, how you're measuring those roles is going to be very important to the success of your venture.

The framework for ultimate persuasion is best summed up by Blair Warren: "People will do anything for those who encourage their dreams, justify their failures, allay their fears, confirm their suspicions, and help them throw rocks at their enemies."[1]

If you look at your entire sales process through that lens, you cannot help but have an absolutely perfected sales process. If your sales process has each of these key areas, it's going to, as Dan Sullivan would say, get people "intellectually engaged in a future result that is good for them" and get them to "emotionally commit to take action to achieve that result."[2]

At Kajabi, this was a unique process. Like many software companies, we didn't have a sales arm because our process was more self-selection. At Kajabi, even with Promotion and Persuasion being integrated, it didn't negate the importance for both roles to deliver their requirements. We needed to have a marketing process that essentially canned and cloned the salesperson and built that salesperson into every presentation we were giving through a marketing funnel.

The way we did that was by being very clear about where the marketing aspects started and where the sales process started. And for us, the marketing process was getting the interest, getting the click, and getting a prospect enrolled in exploring further. The sales process then began with the showcasing of customer stories and product capabilities.

Now in your business, sales may be a very different amplifier for you. Persuasion may live in a very different role. This is where I want you to be very clear that if all you get here is the clarity and the difference between roles, it's going to be very impactful for your business.

---

1   Goodreads. "Blair Warren Quotes." *Goodreads, Inc*, 2024. https://www.goodreads.com/author/quotes/474867.Blair_Warren.

2   Greene, Mike. "The Best Salesperson Is Defined by Something Greater than the Latest Transaction." *The Business Journals*, March 7, 2021. https://www.bizjournals.com/bizjournals/how-to/marketing/2014/01/what-is-selling.html.

Keep in mind as you think about your current business:

- Are you asking salespeople to play the role of marketing?
- Are you asking marketing to play the role of sales?
- Are sales accountable for both leads and sales, or are those roles split between a business development representative and an account executive?

Clarifying Persuasion KPIs and understanding what your decision drivers are—whether in your own business or a business you're interested in investing in—is a critical amplifying component to increase the size of your Billion Dollar Bullseye.

What Is Persuasion?

Persuasion and marketing are related concepts, but they have different meanings and goals. Marketing is the process of identifying, promoting, and distributing a message to a target market with the goal of generating leads and/or sales. The main goal of marketing is to create awareness and interest in the product or service being offered and to persuade potential customers to take a step toward buying it. Whether brand or direct response in nature, marketing is designed to capture the attention of your target market and direct the already present desires toward the appropriate next action.

Marketing is the art of aggregating and directing attention.

Persuasion, on the other hand, is the art of convincing someone to change their beliefs or behaviors. It involves influencing people to take a specific action, adopt a particular attitude, or change their perception of a product or service.

Persuasion can be used to encourage customers to buy a product, but it can also be used for a variety of other purposes, such as motivating employees, gaining support for a cause, or building relationships with customers.

In short, when it comes to building your Billion Dollar Bullseye, marketing is the art of getting attention. Persuasion is the art of driving action and commitment.

This is sales, but not in the traditional sense.

Hard selling is no longer effective; people are not receptive to aggressive tactics. Instead, they seek meaningful conversations, solutions, partnerships, connections, a sense of belonging to tribes, and the feeling of being part of a community. Even skilled car salesmen have shifted away from the traditional "selling" approach, embracing a more consultative style.

Persuading someone to buy requires an understanding of the customer's needs, wants, and desires, as well as what drives their decision-making process. To persuade effectively, businesses need to craft a compelling message that speaks to the customer's pain points and highlights the benefits of the product or service being offered. This can be done through various marketing channels such as advertising, social media, email marketing, or content marketing.

Effective persuasion also involves establishing trust with the customer, which can be achieved through social proof, customer testimonials, and positive reviews. It's important to provide the customer with all the information they need to make an informed decision and to be transparent about any potential downsides or risks associated with the product or service.

Ultimately, the goal is to create a sense of urgency (more on this in a bit) and motivate the customer to take action by making the purchasing process as easy and straightforward as possible.

Take a moment to examine some of these persuasive practices and the mistakes businesses make.

When Companies Fail to Persuade

#1 Fail: False urgency or scarcity

From your own experience on planet Earth, you know how this can go wrong. A few years ago, the whole idea of urgency and scarcity was a core component of Persuasion. *Make them think they'll never get it if they don't get it now, now, NOW!*

Yeah, people got tired of that pretty quickly.

Creating false urgency in the persuasion process leads to strong negative consequences for both the business and the customer. If the customer feels like they are being pressured into making a purchase, they will end up feeling resentful or manipulated. This can damage the trust and relationship between the customer and the business. Additionally, if the customer ends up making a purchase they later regret because of the false urgency, then you get returns or negative reviews which harm your business's reputation.

Moreover, if a business repeatedly creates false urgency in its promotions, it creates a pattern of behavior that customers may eventually recognize and stop trusting. This can lead to long-term damage to the company's reputation and bottom line. It's essential to use honest and ethical persuasion tactics to build strong and lasting relationships with customers.

And when it comes to scarcity, that's almost a non-starter. If you're running a software company, your "thing" doesn't run out! It's like telling people they'd better buy an eBook fast, or it'll run out. It won't. Remember those campaigns with a certain number of "digital downloads" remaining? Yeah, me too.

Be honest and real when it comes to urgency and scarcity. You'll be surprised how annoyed people will get when they feel they're being pressured into a buy, and they will often not make the purchase on principle, even if they really want it.

In 2023, two Washington consumers filed a proposed class action lawsuit against clothing retailer Old Navy, accusing the company of spamming them with misleading emails regarding the duration of sales.[3] The plaintiffs claimed that some emails falsely advertised products as being on sale for only "today" or "this week," yet the following day (or week), they received emails promoting the same sale. Additionally, certain emails claimed that customers had a final opportunity to avail themselves of a discount, but subsequently, the plaintiffs received emails advertising the same discount. The plaintiffs also received emails stating that a sale with a set deadline had been "extended" shortly after receiving initial communication about it. As of the publication of this book, that lawsuit has not yet been resolved. Regardless, it's a bad look for any clothing retailer, especially one marketed toward families.

Another example of a company that failed because of false urgency in its marketing is the Fyre Festival.[4] The festival was marketed as a luxurious, once-in-a-lifetime event that was going to take place on a private island in the Bahamas. The marketing campaign emphasized exclusivity and urgency, telling customers that tickets were selling out quickly and creating a sense of FOMO (fear of missing out) among potential attendees.

However, the festival turned out to be a disaster. Attendees arrived to find that the luxurious accommodations promised in the marketing were actually disaster relief tents, and many of the promised performers and attractions were nowhere to be found. The festival was ultimately canceled, and the organizers were charged with fraud.

The Fyre Festival is a prime example of the dangers of false urgency in marketing. By creating a sense of urgency and exclusivity that was not based

3   Winston, Aaron R. "Old Navy Class Action Lawsuit Settlement: What's Going On?" *Express Legal Funding*, November 5, 2023. https://expresslegalfunding.com/old-navy-lawsuit-settlement/.
4   Huddleston Jr., Tom. "Fyre Festival: How a 25-Year-Old Scammed Investors out of $26 Million." *CNBC Make It*, August 2019. https://www.cnbc.com/2019/08/18/how-fyre-festivals-organizer-scammed-investors-out-of-26-million.html.

in reality, the festival organizers were ultimately unable to deliver on their promises and left many customers feeling cheated and betrayed.

Then, there's the clothing retailer Abercrombie & Fitch. In 2003, the company was accused of artificially limiting supply to create a sense of scarcity and exclusivity in its products.[5] Abercrombie & Fitch was found guilty of withholding certain clothing sizes from its stores to create the impression that they were in high demand, even though they were readily available in their warehouses. As a result, the company faced legal action and negative publicity, which damaged its reputation and caused customers to lose trust in the brand.

Bottom line, people don't like to be played. Don't do it.

#2 Fail: Lies, damn lies!

Social media, reviews, and testimonials seem like no-brainers in the art of persuasion, but thanks to a few truth-benders, this pond has been tainted.

It used to be that people looked for testimonials and reviews and made purchasing decisions based on other people's experiences. But when companies started to post fake reviews and testimonials, people stopped knowing who to trust, so they now take reviews with a pinch of salt.

One high-profile example is the company Lifestyle Lift, which was sued by the New York State Attorney General's office in 2009 for publishing fake consumer reviews on websites such as RealSelf.com and CitySearch.com.[6]

---

5   Warren, Liz. "Abercrombie & Fitch Documentary Revisits Its Discriminatory History." Rivet, Sourcing Journal, April 14, 2022. https://sourcingjournal.com/denim/denim-business/abercrombie-fitch-white-hot-netflix-documentary-discrimination-hiring-size-inclusivity-338646/.
6   Cain Miller, Claire. "Company Settles Case of Reviews It Faked." *New York Times*, July 14, 2009. https://www.nytimes.com/2009/07/15/technology/internet/15lift.html.

The company agreed to pay $300,000 in fines and to stop publishing fake reviews.

In another case, the skincare company, Sunday Riley, was found to have encouraged employees to write fake positive reviews on Sephora's website to boost sales.[7] The company settled with the Federal Trade Commission in 2019 and agreed to stop posting fake reviews and to disclose any incentivized reviews.

Consequences for this sort of skullduggery aren't small. The FTC (Federal Trade Commission) took action against Lumosity, a brain training app, for using deceptive advertising, including using fabricated testimonials in their ads. Lumosity paid a $2M settlement as a result.[8]

It all comes down to reputation in the end. If customers don't trust the reviews, they don't trust the company, which is why Amazon is merciless in its hunt for fake reviews. They'll use everything from AI to human intervention, purchase validation to reviewer ranking, and ultimately, their "Vine Voices," which is an invitation-only review process.

If you don't have reviews or testimonials yet, do some of the following:

1. **Ask for reviews from existing customers:** Reach out to your existing customers and request them to leave a review on your website or on third-party review sites. You can make this process easier by sending a follow-up email after a purchase, including a call to action that links to the review site.
2. **Leverage social proof:** Even if you don't have many reviews yet, you can still showcase other types of social proof, such as the number

---

7   Mcspadden, Kevin. "You Now Have a Shorter Attention Span than a Goldfish." *Time*, May 14, 2015. https://time.com/3858309/attention-spans-goldfish/.

8   Federal Trade Commission. "Lumosity to Pay $2 Million to Settle FTC Deceptive Advertising Charges for Its 'Brain Training' Program." *Federal Trade Commission*, January 5, 2016. https://www. ftc.gov/news-events/news/press-releases/2016/01/lumosity-pay-2-million-settle-ftc-deceptive-advertising-charges-its-brain-training-program.

of customers served, awards won, or endorsements from trusted sources in your industry.

3. **Offer incentives:** Offering a small incentive, such as a discount or a free trial, can encourage customers to leave a review. Just be sure to disclose that you're offering an incentive in exchange for the review.

4. **Build relationships:** By building strong relationships with your customers and delivering an exceptional experience, you can encourage them to become brand ambassadors and leave positive reviews or testimonials.

5. **Utilize case studies:** Use case studies to showcase the positive experiences of your existing customers. This can help potential customers better understand the value of your product or service and build trust in your brand.

Just don't lie or mislead. EVER.

#3 Fail: Confusing persuasion with pushy

When salespeople push too hard and come across as too aggressive or insincere, it turns off potential customers and damages the reputation of the company. Customers feel like they are being manipulated or pressured into making a purchase, which can leave a bad taste in their mouths, and they're likely to seek out competitors instead.

A pushy sales team may focus solely on closing deals in the short term without taking into account the long-term needs of the customer or building a relationship with them. As you can imagine, this leads to a high turnover of customers and a lack of repeat business, which will ultimately hurt the growth and sustainability of your business.

To avoid this, it's important for sales teams to focus on building relationships with customers and providing them with value rather than solely on closing deals. By taking the time to understand the customer's needs and concerns, and providing them with relevant information and solutions, a sales team can build trust and loyalty, leading to long-term growth and success for the business.

When people feel like they are being pushed into a sale, they become defensive and skeptical, and may even feel manipulated or exploited. This will lead to distrust and a negative image of the salesperson and the business.

Pushy sales tactics will create an uncomfortable experience for the customer (which does not contribute to the prestigious experience you want your customers to have), making them feel like they are being taken advantage of or pressured. As a result, they may leave without making a purchase, or they may make a purchase and then regret it later, leading to negative reviews, returns, and reduced customer loyalty. Ultimately, pushy sales tactics will harm your reputation, hinder growth, and limit future opportunities for building strong customer relationships.

This is an undeniable truth: Always treat people with respect and recognize their intelligence. If you don't view them as deserving of respect or as intelligent, why would you want them in your business in the first place?

Persuasion does not equal pushy. Full stop.

How to Make It Work

Persuasion is the art of convincing someone to change their beliefs or take a specific action. (In this case, coming into the world your solution provides them.) While there are many different strategies and techniques for persuasion we could talk about ad nauseum, there are several key principles that are often cited as essential to the process.

The key tenets of Persuasion are:

1. **Ethos:** The credibility and trustworthiness of the person or organization making the argument. Persuasion is more effective when the person making the argument is perceived as knowledgeable, experienced, and trustworthy. Having a strong purpose ties into ethos. Do you want to help the environment? Do your customers care about sustainability? You'll boost your ethos and credibility by taking actions that back up your green goals. You'll know if you've nailed this because it results in nearly no selling being required. People simply ask to buy.
2. **Logos:** The use of logic and reason to make an argument, aka what most people try and fail miserably to do. Persuasion often involves presenting a logical and compelling case for why someone should believe or do something. Given that we are creatures who buy with emotion and justify with logic, save the logos for the justification process to tie off your persuasion instead of using logos right out the gate. Without the emotional commitment, the logic to justify isn't needed nor is it helpful.
3. **Pathos:** The use of emotions to persuade, aka where you should start with persuasion when it's your turn to speak—after you've listened and listened and listened some more. Persuasion involves appealing to the emotions of the other person, and there are so many ways to do this that aren't icky, creepy, or manipulative. Think of storytelling or vivid language to create an emotional connection. Remember to tread carefully because, if done authentically, emotions are what drive the human experience, but if manipulated, they create lasting scorn for the manipulator.
4. **Audience:** Aka, listening to your market. Persuasion is more effective when it is tailored to the needs and interests of the audience. I see businesses go kaput when they try to tailor their messaging to *everyone* as opposed to their specific audience. You try to make supper with too many cooks in the kitchen, and your message is either too bland to attract anyone or way too adventurous a concoction to be on any sane person's menu. Successful persuasion

requires an understanding of the other person's perspectives, beliefs, and motivations.

5. **Timing:** You know how you're more likely to agree to a favor asked of you if you're allowed to finish your coffee first? Persuasion is more effective when it is timed correctly. It may be more effective to make a persuasive argument when the other person is in a positive mood or receptive to new ideas. This requires the core skill of persuasion that I'm sure you haven't heard enough yet—listening.

   Driving this home even further, you've likely heard the maxim, "Pioneers get the arrows and settlers get the land." Timing is the difference between this evening's salad and tomorrow's garbage. This is an area that must be carefully calibrated with your market. Its current level of awareness and ignoring it can kill a business before it even starts.

6. **Consistency:** Persuasion is more effective when it is consistent with the other person's existing beliefs and values. Arguments that are inconsistent with the other person's beliefs may be more difficult to accept. Oftentimes, there are belief shifts that need to happen in your customers before they're ready to hop over the fence into your world. You achieve these subtle shifts and ultimate consistency by—you guessed it—listening and ethos. Not to mention that today, the average human attention span is less than that of a goldfish (seriously[9]), so repetition is a must.

7. **Call to action:** Persuasion involves a call to action, encouraging the other person to take a specific action. You have to ask them to dance. You'll never know how they feel if you don't say anything. The call to action should be clear, concise, and compelling. Anything without some call to action is a complete waste. A confused mind never buys, so if you're waiting for your audience to arrive at a buying decision without telling them, you'll definitely run out of money before customers run out of options.

---

9   Mcspadden, "You Now Have a Shorter Attention Span."

That's all very well, but how would that look in action?

You'd start with your audience because, let's be honest, they're probably not that interested in you. They just want their problem solved.

1. **Audience:** What do they need? What are they interested in? Consider their existing beliefs, values, and motivations, and listen well because everything you say will need to speak to all that and any other concerns they have.
2. **Pathos:** Use emotional appeals to connect with your audience on a deeper level. A genuine interest in what they've just told you goes a long way.
3. **Ethos:** This is all about trust. Your customers need to know that you know what you're doing. Reeling off years of experience, number of customers, stats, and awards will do very little. Answering their questions clearly and concisely without guff or spin, in a way they can understand and implement, goes a long way. While you're doing this, spin back to Pathos every now and then by including a story from other customers who were trying to achieve the same thing. Frame it as "This other guy had the same question/issue as X, and we worked with him to do Y and he got Z result."
4. **Logos:** When you're connected and they trust you, you can start using logic and rational arguments to discuss their needs and wants in relation to your product or service. This is where you include evidence, proof, case studies, and anything else that will strengthen your potential customers' faith in you.
5. **Timing:** Don't rush, push, bully, or coerce. Just don't. It's not worth it. Even if they buy, it'll be with a hint of distaste.
6. **Consistency:** Throughout the whole conversation, build your argument on a foundation of existing beliefs and values that your audience shares. Find common ground and emphasize points of agreement before moving on to more controversial or challenging ideas. Repeat as needed.
7. **Call to action:** End with a clear and compelling call to action,

encouraging your audience to take a specific step or make a specific decision based on your persuasion. Make it easy for them to take action by providing clear instructions and support.

In this context, let's talk a little about curiosity.

Curiosity is a crucial element of persuasion and negotiation. It allows you to gather more information about the other party's interests and motivations, which will help you find a solution that satisfies your client or customer. Curiosity is what will keep you listening to your prospect well after any cultivated manners have run out.

Sales go wrong when the salesperson isn't curious enough because they're too focused on their own goals and priorities and don't take the time to truly understand the client's perspective. By cultivating curiosity and asking real, honest, open-ended, genuine questions (not a list of questions off a sheet they've been handed by someone who's never taken a call), the salesperson can gather more information and build rapport, which is more likely to lead to a close where everyone is happy.

The added benefit of being open and honestly curious is the salesperson is less likely to make assumptions or jump to conclusions about the customer's motivations, needs, or wants. How infuriating is it when someone launches into an argument against something you aren't even saying? Nothing begets disconnection like a lack of listening and curiosity, or worse yet, interrupting to get to the next line of a script.

By staying curious and open-minded, your team can avoid misunderstandings and work toward a mutually beneficial solution. And when people buy with that frame of mind, they tend to stick around for the long haul, which can only be good for your profit circle because that's when people become repeat buyers and worth more to your company year after year.

The Power of a Great Conversation

One of the failings of most books on sales is the overcomplication of the sales process. The bottom line is connection. It's what you get wherever you have a great conversation.

In order to have a great conversation, there are several key tenets that you need to keep in mind. These include authenticity, open-mindedness, empathy, respect, clarity, and engagement. That doesn't mean you can't have a fun personality. God knows I've got a smart mouth, but I know when to use it and when to shut up.

Listen like it matters, you care, and you are interested. They call it active listening, but really, it's being interested in the person you're speaking to. Pay attention, ask questions to clarify points, and show interest in their perspective. By actively listening, you can gain a deeper understanding of the other person's thoughts and feelings. And when people feel heard and understood, they want to stick around. We like to buy and want to buy from people we like.

It's easier to listen like you care when you're being real. Authenticity, being true, and expressing what you honestly think and feel will take your conversation to another level. This is why it's important your sales team actually believes in what you do! The customer on the other end of the line is not an idiot. They will spot disingenuity a mile off, and they'll slow and eventually stop the conversation because that feeling they get is the same one they get when they're being lied to. So ... be real. Take in their viewpoints and opinions, even if they differ from your own. This will help foster mutual understanding and respect.

Through all that, speak from the heart. **Empathy** will help you understand the other person you're speaking to. If your solution will solve problems, you need to know and feel what it's like to have that problem.

All this leads to two-way **respect**—you for the customer and the customer for you. Never belittle or dismiss their ideas or feelings.

When you're in their corner and they know it, you can help take the whole conversation a step further by **keeping things clear** by avoiding jargon or technical language. Keep checking in to make sure they fully understand what you're saying and what they're buying.

You know what it's like to have a great conversation. It's one that leaves you feeling enriched, educated, informed, amused, and connected. You remember the people you have great conversations with.

So ... you're curious, you're interested, and you've got the whole open-question thing down, but how do you genuinely listen to the human being you're talking to when, let's be honest, you do have an agenda beyond a great conversation?

You start by not wanting to sell at all. You start by wanting to help.

This is something a buddy of mine calls the "prescriptive sales process." Like a doctor to a patient, you uncover symptoms that let you prescribe a solution.

And you can only help when you really listen. So, how do you really listen and hear another person when your head is full of your own ideas, what you think is good for them, the fact that you want another notch in your sales belt, and that you work on commission, and want a new car ...?

Truly listening to someone is hard. It's easy to let our own thoughts and distractions get in the way of hearing what someone else has to say. And let's be honest, when someone tells you to "just shut off your own thinking and really listen," you get the urge to walk away.

"Just listening" is hard. Listening with the intention of finding out how you can help is a different story.

When you *really* want to help someone—I'm not talking about the swoop-in, rescue, hero with a cape stuff. I'm talking about giving someone what they really need, not what you think they need—what do you naturally do?

It looks a little something like this:

1. **You're in the moment.** You are watching and listening not only for what they say but what they're not saying. You're focusing on their pauses, their words, their tone, and their pace. You can hear certainty and uncertainty. You can hear doubt and fear, worries and concerns. You're putting your own feelings aside, so you have space to feel theirs.

2. **You don't interrupt.** You know that the moment you interrupt someone, they will shut down, hesitate, and forget what they said. It will stop a conversation cold in its tracks. How do you know they've finished saying what they want to say and aren't just pausing to think? You often don't, which is why you need to slow down and give the conversation space. Kinda like you're on a beach with a buddy, and you're both watching the waves roll in and aren't in a hurry to get anywhere. Let there be space between words. You'll find your customer has far more to say when they're not feeling pushed, rushed, or talked over.

3. **Listen for all the cues.** People won't say what they mean, especially if they're feeling concerned or on the edge of a purchase that might be stretching them. Listen for those cues where you know what they're really saying when they're just not using their words.

4. **Keep your questions open** to encourage them to talk more. Let me put it this way: If you analyze your conversation and you're doing more than 30% of the talking, then you're talking too much.

5. **Don't judge.** People will shut down, switch off, and hang up the moment they feel judged.

I hope you can see the trend here. Persuasion isn't about selling. It's about helping. It's about being a human being and helping another human being solve a problem in their lives.

So, Who Gets It Right?

1. **Apple** is a master at persuasive marketing. They use carefully designed launch plans to create a sense of exclusivity and anticipation around their product releases, which builds hype and excitement.

   The draw of being in an exclusive club + anticipation of innovation + hype + excitement = Persuasion

2. **Nike's** use of emotion and storytelling makes for powerful persuasion. Their images, videos, and slogans create a sense of deep motivation and empowerment. Celebrity endorsements go a long way in creating social proof and credibility.

   Motivation + empowerment + social proof = Persuasion

3. **Amazon** is an avid protector of their review system and is merciless when people try to cheat it. The result is, for the most part, these reviews can be trusted as honest and transparent, which gives Amazon customers confidence in their purchase.

   Trust + transparency + confidence = Persuasion

4. **Coca-Cola** goes all out to capture Disney/Hollywood-style fantasies in every one-minute ad. Happiness, nostalgia, bright colors, and catchy music are all designed to make people simply want to join in. They were the original creators of "FOMO."

   Positive emotions + great aesthetics + FOMO (fear of missing out) = Persuasion

5. **Old Spice** is the class clown you want to be friends with. They use humor, creativity, witty and outlandishly funny commercials, social media campaigns, and packaging to create a sense of fun and excitement. They drive it home with celebrity endorsements to create social proof and credibility.

   Humor + longevity + celebrity endorsements (social proof) = Persuasion

6. If Old Spice is the class clown, **Red Bull** is the amped-up jock fit to take on any dare for a dollar. They use extreme sports, music, and events to create a sense of adrenaline and excitement.

   Tribe mentality + permission to be wild = Persuasion

7. **CarMax** is the antithesis of the used car salesman. Buying a used car no longer involves hard sales tactics and feeling pushed around. Their no-haggle pricing strategy eliminates the traditional negotiation process, which makes buying a car feel like a battle you're going to lose. Quality assurance and a seven-day return policy are pretty great at putting the buyer at ease.

   Treating the customer as an equal + transparency + space for the customer to change their mind = Persuasion

Overall, these companies are great at persuasion because they create a sense of emotion, exclusivity, social proof, and personalization. They understand their target audience and use persuasive techniques to create a connection and influence their behavior.

Do you notice the same companies keep coming up? Over and over? When you get the rings of the bullseye right, you get it ALL right!

There's a lot of ignorance and more than a few misconceptions about selling that prevent people from achieving sales success. There are also some foundational concepts around selling that, if you fail to understand and appreciate, you'll experience significant frustration, anxiety, and other negative emotions about selling. If you have a complete understanding of sales, you'll understand that sales are a way to serve others, demonstrate leadership, and demonstrate a deep commitment to your goals and purpose in life.

You have to understand both the customer's needs and the company's products or services. You have to build trust with customers and commit to developing a sales approach based on building long-term relationships rather than simply closing transactions.

Over the years, these are the core principles I stick to:

1. **You must understand your customer's needs and desires.** You have to listen and be willing to ask questions and dig deeper to get a full understanding of what the customer is looking for.
2. **You have to provide real value.** This means demonstrating a deep understanding of the customer's needs and providing solutions that meet those needs in a meaningful way.
3. **You must work on a foundation of trust.** You do that by being transparent, honest, and reliable.
4. **Whenever you sell anything, focus on the long term.** This isn't a fling. You want a long relationship with your customers. That means you have to know, like, and trust each other. This requires a deep understanding of the customer's needs and a commitment to providing ongoing value over time.
5. **You've got to be adaptable.** The best salespeople are able to adapt to changing circumstances and customer needs. This requires being nimble and flexible and being able to quickly pivot in response to changing market conditions or customer demands.

These principles can be applied in any industry or market.

By prioritizing customer understanding, delivering tangible value, nurturing trust, emphasizing long-term relationships, and remaining adaptable, you will cultivate successful and enduring partnerships with your customers, propelling meaningful growth in their businesses.

Take Aim …

Successful persuasion is the ability to influence others and get them to take a desired action. This skill is essential for building successful businesses, attracting customers, partners, and investors, and achieving really anything you want in life. Unless you live on an island with goldfish for company, you're going to need to develop this and make sure your sales team masters it too.

It's not about manipulation or deception. It's about understanding the other person's perspective. It involves aligning your message to the interests and needs of the other person rather than just pushing your own agenda. By understanding the other person's perspective, you can find a solution that works for both parties and builds long-lasting relationships. And that might not mean a sale right off the bat!

The most effective form of persuasion is through stories and examples that illustrate the benefits of taking the step, making the purchase, and jumping into your offer. Stories are what make you relatable. It's what people connect with.

Part of the process is building trust and rapport. You do that by listening. Honestly listening. Not having some script your team works off where they don't give the customer a moment to think (even though I'm a huge fan of scripts). Show empathy and genuine interest. With that in place, you'll build a real connection and create a sense of mutual understanding.

Human beings are basically self-centered creatures. It takes practice to develop this level of empathy. You get better through practice and feedback. It's a skill you can learn and hone.

Time to See Where Your Dart Lands

1. Take a look at your SALES process, not your marketing and awareness process, but your sales process. The things you do to get people to hand over their money. Review it. Is it too pushy? Are there a ton of refund requests? Is it easy for the sales team or are they struggling to get people over the line?
2. Compare your sales process to at least one of the companies that are nailing Persuasion. How do you measure up? Where can you optimize?
3. While you do that, add a little Prestige. How can you turn your sales process into a red-carpet experience?

_____

_____

_____

_____

_____

_____

_____

_____

Once again, do yourself a favor and take the time to stop and think about your business, your sales process, and what it's like for your customers to buy from you.

Answer "YES" or "NO" to the questions below:

Statement	Y/N
Your sales team closes at least 30% of the calls they receive (or is surpassing industry benchmarks).	
Your refund rate is less than 2% (or is below industry benchmarks).	
People are ready to buy when they call because they know and understand what you can do for them. You don't have a lot of missed appointments or no-shows.	
If someone isn't a good fit for your business, you say no and tell them what they need before they can buy your product or service.	
Your sales team enjoys their work! The turnover is low, and the engagement is high.	
Your sales team is looped into the product development team, so they know what's in the pipeline.	
Your sales team is made up of people who like people!	
Your sales team is fully trained in all aspects of the business and has a line into product development based on what people say and ask for during the sales process.	
You've mystery-shopped the sales process and loved it!	
You spot problems in your team's performance and deal with them fast.	

For the statements you answered "YES" to, make sure it's a good, honest "yes," then go see where you can improve.

For any statements you answered "NO" to, take time to make sure you've nailed every other ring of the bullseye coming to this point. If you're struggling to close sales calls, it means another ring of the bullseye is missing or not fully developed. If every circle prior to this is optimized, then sales is as easy as people calling up and saying yes.

How to Know You've Hit the Persuasion Target

At Kajabi, we optimized Persuasion by blending it with Promotion. Let me explain. We had the opportunity to have a lot of our marketing done in a way that would best be called a "case study"—showcasing the achievements of our customers. This gave us the ability to tell stories about specific customers who were operating in specific universes, whether it be health and fitness, personal development, career skills, sports, cooking, etc.

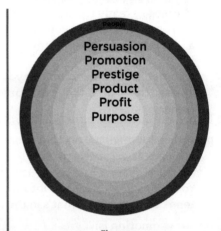

Figure 9

The Expanded Bullseye: Purpose through Persuasion

We could look at a successful customer and talk about what they did or what they loved about our product. So, for us, it was about education-based marketing, namely, showing our market what was possible. And while using education-based marketing and showing them what was possible, we were also able to use their story as social proof.

Education and social proof became our sales process, leveraging achieved outcomes from customer success stories to show what Kajabi can and could do.

You'll know you've hit this target when your product is selling itself through referrals, customer success stories, and education-based marketing.

How Persuasion Ties into People

We're heading to the seventh and final circle of the Bullseye Formula.

People.

Some would argue that people are the most important element of the business, and they'd be wrong.

If your **Purpose** isn't clear, people won't be pulled to your mission.

If your **Profit** isn't nailed, you won't be able to pay them what they're worth.

If your **Product** isn't extraordinary, or at the very least, exactly fit for Purpose, then there will be nothing to support, market, or sell.

If your **Prestige** isn't excellent, then the people you hire will spend their days dealing with complaints and they won't stick around.

If your **Promotion** isn't great, then you won't have an audience, and your amazing people will be sitting around with time on their hands.

If your **Persuasion** isn't naturally brilliant, then you won't have any customers.

You only get **People** if all the rest is in place. Spoiler alert: The best people only want to work with the best companies.

But you're here, and you've nailed the other rings, so let's talk about the ultimate amplifier ... People.

Chapter 8

Ring #7: People

Great teams are not created with incentives, procedures, and perks. They are created by hiring talented people who are adults and want nothing more than to tackle a challenge, and then communicating to them, clearly and continuously, about what the challenge is.

—Patty McCord

And finally, People.

The placement of people in the last ring of the target is probably one of my more controversial perspectives. There have been a bajillion and one books written on hiring talent, maintaining talent, and having only top performers. What I have found is that almost every single interviewing system, every personality profile, and every process that somebody tells me they have perfected for getting great people is always inconsistent.

How many times have you seen some form of "Hire A-players," or "It's all about the people," or "If you just get great people, great things happen," or "Look after your people and they will look after you," or "Your employees are family"?

That's where the strategy surrounding People normally lives ... and dies.

Patty McCord is the only person who said it honestly, "True and abiding happiness in work comes from being deeply engaged in solving a problem with talented people you also know are deeply engaged in solving it and knowing that the customer loves the product or service you have worked so hard to make."[1]

What that means is this: Talent strategy can be boiled down to simplicity. All A-players want to work with other A-players and not be hassled. That's it. A-players are probably going to be excited and drawn in by your vision, assuming you're purposing in public and putting it on display.

If you, as a business owner, are expecting to hire talented people to fix your dumpster fires, it will never ever happen. Talented people know how to assess a dumpster fire very quickly and how to leave very quickly. They're not going to come in and fix your problems.

Your team will only shine as bright or perform as well as the quality of the stage you put them on and the quality of the audience for which they perform. It's why missing any of the rings of your bullseye will damage or destroy your ability to hire great people. People comes last for a reason.

If we go all the way back to the very beginning of the Bullseye Formula, I shared that I grossly underestimated the needs of my business and I put burdens on other departments to fix those needs.

I fell down the rabbit hole of focusing on people as my fix. I was caught in a constant loop saying, "Well, man, if we can just hire the right people, they'll fix this."

Not true. Because the right people are always looking at a business and asking, "What are their systems like? Do they have Purpose? Do they have Profit? Is their Product in alignment? Have they figured out Prestige? Have they nailed Promotion? Have they nailed Persuasion?"

If you haven't nailed any of these and an A-player is looking at your company, they're not going to work for you because they don't want to fix something.

---

1   Quotefancy. "Patty McCord Quotes." *Quotefancy*, 2024. https://quotefancy.com/patty-mccord-quotes.

They want to be engaged in solving problems for your customers—they want to amplify a great business.

An A-player wants to show up and stand on the shoulders of giants. They recognize that no matter how good they are, they will only be as good as the stage they perform on.

That wasn't something I realized until it was far too late. I thought I could fix my people strategy by just getting better people. And what I realized is that every person I hired looked way better if I put them into a system that actually produced results.

Here's what this failure looked like at Kajabi.

Repeatedly, out of a desire to reward people or from the fallacy of wanting more for people than they wanted for themselves, we would over-title. If we needed a C-level hire in any department, we'd look at the most senior employee in that area, slap a new title on them, and send them on their way.

We never stopped to ask, "Does this person have C-level skills? Can they lead a team? Do they even know what we expect from them in this new role?" We just promoted (and compensated) and moved along.

As you can imagine, this led to a myriad of problems. And in some cases, things became very awkward. Not only have you over-titled and overcompensated but it's really all your (the hiring manager's) fault.

What saved Kajabi was that our three core rings were dialed in. We led well with Purpose, purposing in public very effectively. We had teams that were excited and energized by the success of our user base, and they saw themselves as having an opportunity to participate in something bigger than themselves.

But it took a lot of trial and error before we were able to nail People, and most of our success in People came as a result of our success in the previous six areas of the Bullseye Formula.

The reason People is my outermost ring of the Bullseye Formula is because it's the hardest ring to systemize. If you're depending on people as your sole or most important strategy, you're going to be extremely frustrated because you're also going to find that there are just not that many A-players out there. To try and get A-players all of the time is not a reality. However, you can turn people into A-players by being proactive in creating robust and successful systems.

This is why people drive systems.

If you think about business through the lens of systems, you're golden. Let systems inform your strategy for people.

I saw this in my work with Kajabi. We learned a lot by fixing systems rather than fixing people ... but it wasn't always that way for Kajabi. So, how did we survive and succeed despite not having the right people (aka systems) or strategy to begin with?

We nailed Purpose, Profit, and Product. We had our core down tight. That gave us a lot of room to adjust and grow. It allowed us to learn the amplifiers on a solid foundation.

By nailing the three foundational elements and as many amplifiers as possible, you give yourself the time and space to figure the rest out.

So, what do you do now that you know you need to focus more on systems than on people?

Hire slow. Fire fast. The longest period in any manager's life is the time between when he knows someone needs to go and when he actually fires the person, and it is always longer than it should be. In fact, it's longer than everybody wants it to be, including the person you're probably going to fire because they know they're doing a bad job too.

I can't tell you how many times I see business owners missing the mark because they are not willing to give people an exit.

We started doing something at Kajabi. It's actually a term coined by Netflix—kudos to them—called the "good goodbye."

A "good goodbye" isn't disciplinary. It's not a strategy to have a PIP (performance improvement plan) and get your employee so depressed that they quit so you don't have to fire them. No, it's a way of saying, "The business has grown in a different direction and has different needs, so we're going to give you a respectable sendoff. We're going to provide you with enough severance so that you're not afraid that you're not going to be able to eat, and we're going to wish you the best."

Initially, it was difficult to implement because severance is expensive! Is that what we really wanted to do? But we quickly found that equipping people to move into their next season was the cheapest force multiplier we could have ever purchased in the company.

The "good goodbye" sounds a little counterintuitive, but it was a win for us at Kajabi.

Culture

Culture is one of those things that you must think about as a business owner today, especially in the wake of the Great Resignation, or even worse, Quiet Quitting. Quite frankly, all of the numbers on Quiet Quitting and the Great Resignation, as scary as they are about employee engagement, are woefully underreported because nobody wants to indicate that they actually hate what they're doing. What that says to me is that there's not a company that people are Quiet Quitting from that doesn't have a mission, vision, and values.

We're confronted with this giant question of what we're going to do with this mess, and the answer we hear is that this mission, vision, and value set are supposed to enroll your team and get everyone excited about rowing in the same direction. We have countless books written on this concept, and yet, here we stand with the most disengaged workforce on the planet. The reality is that the mission-vision-values approach is, at worst, done as a push strategy where you're ramming that doctrine down the throats of your employees—which guarantees they won't care at all.

It doesn't matter how great your mission is or how pure your values are. This approach is not going to solve employee engagement.

It's not even going to work if you crowdsource your mission with your existing team. We've gone into the nitty gritty on this, but if you've forgotten, essentially trying to get buy-in from your team by diluting your original purpose is terrible. You can't make your team care about your purpose if you're pushing them—directly or indirectly—toward your purpose.

The one and only solution is to use a pull strategy. Put your purpose on display. Allow others to raise their hands and opt to be a part of it. This empowers people to go beyond the paycheck and show up, fully engaged in the purpose of your business. (If nobody cares, you may want to reevaluate that mission, vision, and values set.)

In a fun, random metaphor, let's say I want to go join Yellowstone after watching the first five seasons of the show. I know what it looks like to be a cowboy on John Dutton's ranch. I know the bar fights I'm going to get in. I know the guns I'll carry. I know how I'm going to do on the ranch. But at no point in that show did John Dutton monologue his mission, vision, and values to push me into being a cowboy on his ranch. He never did a workshop with everyone at Yellowstone to co-create a mission, vision, or values. It's just there on display, and people get to choose whether they opt in or pass on the opportunity. To me, that is the single leverage point of getting amazingly talented people to fully buy into your purpose and inoculate them against the quiet-quitting plague.

You don't present it. You embody it.

Creating company culture this way does multiple things.

In the early stages, it keeps you as the business owner honest. You're going to be transparent about your journey. You're going to talk about the good, the bad, and the ugly. You're going to share what you're learning, which helps you codify your lessons in a way that helps you not forget. (Remember, the shortest pencil is longer than the longest memory.) And then, when you get your true fans—the people who are on the same page as you in the same book you're writing, the ones who want to keep reading even when it's messy and who are excited by the hyper-growth period—those are the ones who know what they're signing up for. And God willing, they will be the people who then move into the scaling stages with you, assuming they have the appetite.

Keep sharing your purpose publicly, even during this last circle of the bullseye. Draw attention to what you're doing, why you're doing it, and what you're learning, and let your company culture reap the benefits.

In fact, culture and community are the two things no company can duplicate. It's not cookie-cutter. And if you build it right, it will differentiate your company better than anything else you could do. Like Peter Drucker said, "Culture eats strategy for breakfast."[2]

Everyone looks at the competition like they have some secret sauce or edge ... whether that be a unique framework, intellectual property, or the ability to throw money at whatever solution they want.

The truth of the matter is that, in today's day and age, authenticity is currency. Every buying decision is an emotional choice with logical justification. If I identify with that culture and community, I'm going to choose you over them over and over again.

---

2   Guley, Gokhan, and Tracy Reznik. "Culture Eats Strategy for Breakfast and Transformation for Lunch." *The Jabian Journal*, 2019. https://journal.jabian.com/culture-eats-strategy-for-breakfast-and-transformation-for-lunch/#:~:text=The%20core%20tenet%20in%20the,place%20to%20manage%20the%20change.

In this era of AI, genuine human connection will be your distinguishing factor. Publicly express your purpose, share your ongoing learning experiences, and prioritize authenticity. Foster a company culture where people rally behind your success because they understand your values, principles, and the community you serve.

Hiring

A buddy of mine applied the concept of purposing in public and created a number of short, five-minute videos that addressed their journey and what employees could expect from working for his company.

And it's brilliant.

As an employee looking for a job, your potential hire is used to dealing with recruiters. The recruiter gets paid for placing you. There's no care about whether it's the right fit beyond if you have the right skills, right? As an employee, there's a lot of anxiety. What are you getting yourself into? What is the culture really like? Think about all of the points that get glossed over or an underhanded "yes" when really, you start working there, and it was just the company or recruiter telling you what you needed to hear to get the deal.

But to hear all of those things directly from the founder and CEO in a way that is memorialized? Genius. Then, if you as the owner aren't representing what you said in those videos, there's an easy conversation to have. "Hey man, I'm going to need you to go back and watch that video you sent me when I said yes and uprooted my life and family to join your gig because I don't feel like we're sticking to what we agreed on." Done.

I cannot overstate the value, camaraderie, and trust that this tactic engenders if you're willing to be up-front with your hires. Most business owners are guilty of romancing an employee into saying yes without ever really telling them what they're actually in for. We want them to feel like they're going to work in a little, perfectly walled garden. Everyone and everything is absolutely perfect, and they always will be too.

But every employee knows that's not true. It doesn't matter how you package it up. You're a human being running a company that deals with many other human beings. It's not perfect by any stretch of the imagination. And yet, we're still guilty of giving that impression when we go to hire a new team member.

We've got to stop setting up employees to expect a retirement program that's totally chill when we're in hyper-growth mode. Calling back to purposing in public, this is why it is crucial to allow people to opt in.

And I can hear the objections in the back of my mind. No one wants to watch videos, Jonathan. Why would I waste my time? The real question is, do you actually want someone working for you who wouldn't watch a few five-minute videos on your company? What's worse is seeing this response and *still* trying to sell them on why they should join your company. It's insane.

One of my favorite stories of this in action was from Chet Holmes, author of *The Ultimate Sales Machine*. During their process for interviewing salespeople, the interviewer simply said, "I just don't know if I'm really hearing sales superstar right now," and simply paused. You'd be shocked to know how many supposed sales killers simply said, "Oh, okay. Thanks for your time," and hung up. Just being willing to endure a potential moment of awkwardness, the company found out in one interview who would fold like a chair during a sale. Brilliant.

Hiring someone isn't a box to check. Making it as easy as possible to get a new hire into a company is a terrible idea. It creates a future liability and problem if you ever need to downsize.

Instead, my buddy used a different strategy and found the best people for his company. One of them said he made the mistake of watching the videos while on vacation in Mexico. The guy didn't sleep. My buddy had created a vision and opportunity that was so compelling that this potential hire literally couldn't stop thinking about it while he was supposed to be unplugged.

This strategy nails what a good hiring process should look like.

It starts way before the interview. (In fact, in the scenario of the guy on vacation who couldn't stop thinking about these videos my buddy made, there was no interview, *and he was one of the best hires my friend made for his business!*) It starts with the message you put out there and how you choose to communicate with your potential hires.

Most people approach this part of the people equation from a hiring perspective of, "How do we interview?" and, "How do we get the right people on board?"

Then it's a struggle to keep them in your company, to keep them engaged. And God, don't get me started on how many times I hear, "Well, how do we get the mission, vision, and values to resonate more with them to help them understand why they're here in the first place?" Just, no.

The way we approach hiring is a flawed system. It's something that, quite frankly, is too heavy of a lift to ever actually work. Every entrepreneur knows people are important, but what doesn't get enough attention is that people don't join companies for the reasons you're selling them.

A-players want to work with other A-players. That's the simple truth of it. If you're going to try and trick an A-player into joining your team by giving them more money, jamming your mission, vision, and values down their throat, or fooling them in the interview process, it's not going to work.

The only thing that will keep an A-player around is doing work they care about in a company that has thought through what makes the company great … which is why People is the outermost circle.

In order to get great people, you need to nail all of the bullseye rings. Do you know why you exist and who you serve? Are the numbers in your favor to sustain a long-term business? Do you have the commitment to your product? Do you show up for your customers? Did you build effective systems wherein any team member can deliver positive results?

The Problem with People

When people say, "I've got bad Product, bad Prestige, bad Promotion, bad Persuasion, bad everything ... I'm just going to hire great people, and they're going to build me a great company ..." Nope, that's not going to happen. People can be your biggest problem. Maybe you're the one-in-a-billion with a purpose so compelling and profits so strong that you can rely on those to fix everything else, but I've never seen that be the case.

No matter how hard you try, people come with baggage. They'll have days when their motivation is low, they have issues, they're hungover, they're distracted, and they decide they don't like their colleagues or the color of the sky. They might find themselves in trouble and think it's a good idea to bring that trouble to your business. You have no idea the lengths and breadth of human craziness. Emphasis on *human*.

Since humans can be unpredictable, it's wise not to place them at the core of your bullseye. Doing so is the #1 mistake businesses make in regard to people.

#1 Mistake: Relying on people as the center of your bullseye

It's not something you can build a business around. If your strategy is, "I've got a great idea and I'm just going to hire great people," I think you're kind of screwed because you're going to constantly be wondering, "Did I get the right people? Did I get the wrong people?" Looking at what it costs from a wrong-person-being-hired perspective can be painful.

So, this is definitely an element where I think businesses put People at the center because they're reliant on it, but the reality of it is you only need to be reliant on people if you've built poor systems.

For me, that's why the last ring of the bullseye is People because I believe that the people component is the hardest thing to actually depend on or to do predictably.

So many of the business books out there say, "The greatest thing you can do is hire great people and get out of the way." If that strategy really worked, every startup would work, and every company would work because every company does nothing but try and hire talented people.

But the reality of it is that talented people will only shine as brightly as the stage that they're on. If you put a talented person into a dumpster fire, only 1 out of 100 is going to be so excited that they'll fix the dumpster fire. For 99 people out of 100, they're out, or worse yet, never in.

#2 Mistake: Treating hires like family

Treating staff like family may seem like a good idea in theory, but it's a bad idea.

Firstly, treating staff like family can create unrealistic expectations and a sense of entitlement among employees. Family members often help each other out and go the extra mile, but in a business context, this can lead to employees feeling that they are entitled to special treatment, privileges, or benefits. This will result in resentment from other employees who feel that the "family members" are receiving preferential treatment.

Secondly, treating staff like family leads to a lack of professionalism and an overly relaxed working environment. While it's important to build relationships and a positive company culture, treating employees too informally will cause a lack of boundaries and a lack of respect for authority.

As if all that weren't enough, treating staff like family can make it difficult to make tough business decisions. In a family, emotions and personal relationships often cloud decision-making, and the same thing happens in a business where employees are treated like family. If an employee is underperforming or causing problems, it becomes hard to address the issue if the employee is viewed as a family member rather than an employee. After all, you've never been able to fire your weird Uncle Bill, no matter how much you wish you could.

Finally, treating staff like family can create legal and ethical issues. In a family, it's not uncommon to blur the lines between personal and professional relationships, but in a business, this is sure to lead to accusations of favoritism, discrimination, or harassment. It's important for businesses to maintain professional boundaries and treat all employees fairly and equally.

#3 Mistake: Expecting people to come pre-packed with your company know-how

It's not uncommon for companies to expect new hires to quickly understand the way things are done and adapt to the company's culture and processes. This approach will, without exception, lead to issues for you, the company, and said hires.

First off, it's unrealistic. A new hire will join because they have a skill set you need. They don't come branded to your company. They have no idea how you do things around here. Your processes, culture, and expectations are unique to you.

Every company is different, and it takes time for a new employee to learn the ins and outs.

When new employees are expected to know everything right away, it can lead to frustration, confusion, and even anxiety, which can affect their productivity and morale.

As a result, they're going to make mistakes and not feel good about asking questions. Then, because they want to keep their jobs, they're probably going to hide the mistake or blame some sucker down the hall, or worse yet, they will up and quit out of the blue. It's competitive out there, and employees can call the shots. If you hire someone into an unsupportive, unpredictable, and inconsistent environment, don't be surprised when they quest for a different job that treats them better.

In short, expect your hire to know their stuff. Don't expect them to know yours.

How to Make It Work: Using Your Hiring and People as an Amplifier for Great Systems

People, in my opinion, are the ultimate amplifiers, but they are terrible supporters or surrogates for doing the right work in the right areas of this bullseye, especially because people are the most unpredictable and hardest strategic advantage to depend on at scale.

Look at it this way ...

A scalable business (which is what you're building) addresses a large or rapidly growing market and doesn't face significant limitations to growth. Scalable businesses have standardized systems, processes, and procedures that allow them to grow beyond a single owner-operator. This means that employees are trained to follow systems rather than relying on the business owner to make decisions. This is like "idiot-proofing" the business by making it simple enough for people with even modest education, intelligence, or experience to operate.

The key to building amazing teams is building an amazing product and having enough profit to be able to pay them what they're worth. **If you have**

full marks on the other circles, People will naturally follow and amplify the hell out of what you've been building.

If you nail these other systems, those systems only get better with great people. But like Warren Buffett says, "I try to invest in businesses that are so wonderful that an idiot can run them. Because sooner or later, one will."[3]

People should have a strategy that supports great systems and optimizes great systems. People should not be a strategy to supplement or be a surrogate for poorly built systems.

Like Patty McCord said, I believe that "The only thing great people want is to work with great people."[4]

They want to work with great people. They don't want to work with idiots. They want to work with a company that has great systems.

Great salespeople don't want to come into a company with a lackluster sales process. Great marketers don't want to come to a company with lackluster marketing. Great product leaders don't want to come to a company with a lackluster product. Every employee has had an experience where they came to a company that was out of balance. They have felt the stress of needing to be superhuman in their capacity because whatever other capacities are failing are not being addressed.

Before you even contemplate the kind of individuals you want to bring into your company, ensure that all other aspects are meticulously in place. Keep in mind that the performance of your team is directly influenced by the environment you provide them with. It's unfair to talented individuals to onboard them into anything less than a well-organized and thriving business.

---

3   Goodreads. "Warren Buffett Quotes." *Goodreads, Inc*, 2024. https://www.goodreads.com/quotes/3240452-i-try-to-invest-in-businesses-that-are-so-wonderful.
4   McCord, Patty. *Powerful: Building a Culture of Freedom and Responsibility*. United States: Silicon Guild, 2017.

Who Gets This Right?

The best way to find out what works and what doesn't is to look at what other companies do. Accept the fact that people will do the same to you when you head up to and exceed your first billion dollars.

Google

- **Creativity and innovation:** Google encourages its people to be creative, take risks, and try new things. Employees are given 20% of their time (one day a week) to work on projects unrelated to their work that they are passionate about.
- **Work-life balance:** Google knows that if people are torn between work and family, ultimately, work will suffer. To help people feel better about giving their all to the company, Google provides everything from free food to on-site gyms, generous parental leave, and access to wellness programs.
- **Opportunities for growth and development:** Google practices the commonsense belief that if you make your people smarter, they will do better work for you. To that end, they offer on-site classes and training, as well as opportunities to attend conferences and events, knowing it will all come back to help grow the company as a whole.
- **Collaboration:** Unlike the dreaded silo that plagues most large companies, Google goes out of its way to encourage teamwork and collaboration. They use open workspaces and a variety of tools to help people connect and communicate.

Boston Consulting Group

- **Professional development:** Like Google, BCG invests heavily in professional development. The firm has a dedicated career development team that works with employees to help them set and achieve career goals.
- **Culture of mentorship:** At BCG, experienced employees work closely

with junior staff to help them develop the skills and knowledge they
need to succeed.

- **Focus on work-life balance:** Flexible work arrangements, including
  remote work options and sabbaticals, help employees manage their
  personal and professional lives.
- **Collaborative environment:** Practicing what they preach, BCG goes
  to considerable lengths to promote a culture that encourages employees to work together and share knowledge and best practices.
- **Employee engagement:** BCG knows they don't always get it right
  the first time. They regularly seek feedback from employees to identify areas for improvement. Most importantly, they actually listen
  and implement changes that make the firm a better place to work.

BMW

- **Strong corporate culture:** BMW's leadership principles emphasize
  teamwork, innovation, and employee development.
- **Employee development and training:** You can see the trend …
  BMW is another company that invests heavily in employee development and training. This includes formal training programs,
  mentorships, coaching, and opportunities for job rotations and inter-
  national assignments.
- **Employee benefits and perks:** Understanding that competition
  is high, and people move jobs far more easily now than they did before,
  BMW knows they have to make sticking with them worthwhile.
  To do this, they offer benefits like health and wellness programs,
  flexible work arrangements, and opportunities for personal and professional development with on-site amenities like gyms, cafeterias,
  and childcare facilities.
- **Strong leadership:** The company's leaders are committed to creating
  a positive workplace culture and understand that transparency, open
  communication, and collaboration are cornerstones of achieving that
  level of success.

Your People Are Great … What about Your Leaders?

Whether it's just you or you have a team, the leaders in every organization, especially one growing into a billion-dollar business, need to be made of a certain kind of stuff.

You've got to have a clear vision for the future—a crystal clear understanding of where you want to take the organization and what you want to achieve in the long term. That vision must be communicated clearly to the team members in order to inspire them to work toward achieving it.

The people you choose to lead have to be fearless and make the hard decisions, even if they are unpopular. These people understand that difficult decisions are necessary to move the organization forward. Making these decisions takes guts and confidence. Few things will drive away talent faster than a needy, wishy-washy leader.

More importantly, the leaders you choose have to be okay with change. In fact, they've got to see it coming and create the wave. This requires a willingness to embrace new ideas and take calculated risks.

Without exception, your leaders have to be great communicators—or at least have a channel through which they can communicate their ideas, needs, and visions. They must be able to motivate and inspire people, and they have to be able to listen and see a good idea when it comes their way, no matter the source.

They also have to take the personal and professional development of the team to heart. People might be the last ring of the Bullseye Formula, but if you don't take care of them, they can make your world exponentially more difficult.

So, if you are going to be the kind of person who can lead a business to billion-dollar valuations, here are a few things you're going to have to give up, change, or accept:

You don't have all the answers, so you'd better listen. And while you're at it, don't be the leader who takes ideas from your people. They'll stop bringing them, so shut up and listen.

1. Don't threaten people. Threatening only leads to mediocrity. Be obsessed with transparency and providing meaningful feedback. If you have an issue with someone, grow a spine and deal with it fast and face-to-face.
2. Never lie. The truth will always come out.
3. Respect people. Never talk down to them or undermine them.
4. Don't sow seeds of doubt about job security. If they feel insecure, they will leave.
5. Make a healthy work-life balance the standard. A burnt-out team isn't going to achieve anything.
6. Celebrate families, accept that people will sometimes be sick, and expect them to take a vacation!
7. Tie your people's personal goals to everything they do in the organization. When they develop themselves, they'll grow your business.
8. If someone in your business has a side hustle, then let them have it (provided, of course, that they're overachieving in their role)! The whole "you only work for me" thing is old. People have personal goals. Understand that allowing people to pursue their personal goals through their work only inspires them to do their best work.

Here are a few more things you are going to need to give up: expecting to be worshiped, being afraid to be fired (a real risk if your Profit isn't pinned down and you have investors), being afraid of change, acting like an idiotic dictator, and letting your ego run the show.

Take Aim ...

Assuming you have the right processes and systems in place, as well as every other circle of the Bullseye Formula, you still have to take care to gather the right people around you.

If you're hoping to scale your business big, it's going to be challenging, but it's also going to be rewarding. It's going to be fun, but it'll keep you awake at night! You've got to deeply understand that people need to feel valued and appreciated for their contributions. To do that, it's up to you to create a culture that encourages innovation, creativity, and hard work—a culture where development (personal and professional) is recognized as essential.

The fact is that happy employees lead to happy customers, so if you want to have the ultimate in prestigious experience, you've got to have happy employees.

Richard Branson put this so well, "Train people well enough so they can leave, treat them well enough so they don't want to."[5]

If people feel trusted and empowered, they are more likely to take ownership of their work and go above and beyond for their customers.

So, hire for a cultural fit. Make sure the people who join match your values. Make sure collaboration is a strong part of that culture. Create an environment where people are excited about sharing ideas, giving feedback, and working together to achieve the billion-dollar goal. Prioritize your team's well-being. Provide a work environment that supports physical and mental health. And above all, lead by example. You're doing something big here. You have the know-how and the vision. Your people might not have the whole picture. They're following you. Be worth following.

---

5   Branson, Richard. "Your uniqueness is your superpower." *Richard Branson Blog*. Virgin. April 8, 2024. https://www.virgin.com/branson-family/richard-branson-blog/everybody-is-a-genius-in-their-own-wonderful-way.

Time to See Where Your Dart Lands

Look at every member of your team and ask:

- Are they a good fit?
- Are they happy?
- Are they contributing to our growth every day? If not, do yourself and them a favor and give them a "good goodbye." Not letting them go is limiting you and limiting them.

While you do that, do the hard thing and think about your people, your hiring, and your teams. What changes do you need to make?

Answer "YES" or "NO" to the questions below.

Question	Yes or No
When considering the people in your business, does anyone come to mind when you think, "Who just doesn't fit here?"	
Do you do a full review of people in your business on a regular basis?	
Do you hire based on a combination of skill, talent, and personality?	
Do you act quickly (in days) when you recognize someone isn't a good fit?	
Do you listen to the rest of your team and your customers when they mention problems with another team member?	
When mistakes keep happening, do you look to fix your systems and processes first?	
Do you know what your people's goals are?	
Do you have regular conversations with your teams, so you know them and they know you?	
If a stranger were to walk into your business, would they feel a buzz?	

If you want to grow a billion-dollar business, you need to have said "Yes" to every one of these questions. I might have placed them as the last ring on the target, but without them, you won't achieve your goal.

People drive innovation, which is critical if you want to stay ahead of the competition and scale. And innovation doesn't happen in a vacuum. It's driven by the skills, knowledge, and creativity of your people all powered by your purpose.

Although you might set the tone and expectations, people create the culture. A strong, vibrant, smart, exciting culture will attract the talent you need to take the strides (not just steps) you need to make.

And above all, people are the face of your company. You might find yourself on the covers of magazines, on podcasts, or on TV, but your people will be the ones sitting face-to-face with your customers. So, make sure you're all on the same side.

Help Your People Get There

Most people will join your organization with all the practical skills they need and most of the know-how but have a lot of space to grow.

You can either let them grow in a haphazard, random, self-directed way, or you can help them grow in a way that will not only grow your business but will also give them what they want and need.

This brings me to the practice of mentoring.

Having a mentor will help you overcome challenges, learn from someone else's experiences, and achieve your goals faster. I will say that, hands down, I wouldn't have achieved what I have in business without mentors and coaches willing to hold me to a high standard, telling me where I've screwed up, and continually pushing me when I wanted to quit.

Finding a mentor is about seeking out someone who is further along in their career or life journey than you are. It's someone who has the skills, knowledge, and experience to help guide you through the ups and downs. You want to find someone who has walked the path you're walking. Maybe they're not at the end game, but they're much further down the path than you are. They can turn around and shine a light on the internal and external obstacles you're about to face—the same obstacles they have already conquered.

Mentors can provide valuable insights, offer guidance and advice, and share their own personal experiences, helping their mentees grow and develop in ways they might not be able to on their own. Your success is, in part, determined by who you surround yourself with. And having a mentor who has achieved greater heights than you currently have is exactly what you need to hit a Billion Dollar Bullseye.

I also believe that being a mentor is as important as having one. It's more than just giving back. It's about sharing your experiences, skills, and knowledge, shaping the future of your industry, and making a positive impact on the lives of others.

I've been asked countless times, "What's your secret to success?" It's not the hottest new Facebook ad strategy or sneaky webinar script. It's the quality of people you can access at the inevitable inflection points of building your business, what skill matters most at a particular point, what framework you choose for your business, whether you take capital or bootstrap your way to wealth, the price and position of your product in the market, etc. The quality of people you can access during those crossroads is really the only thing that matters. The rest is just a willingness to do the work.

I learned the value of mentors early on. I learned the value of relationships. It's what got me to the right market with the market leader, and it's what got us a $2B valuation at Kajabi. So, build mentoring into your culture, hire leaders who want to mentor their teams, and, as the owner, never stop seeking mentorship and leveling yourself up.

As John Maxwell puts it in the "Law of the Lid," a leader's effectiveness is determined by their ability, and their ability is determined by the limits (or the lid) they place on themselves. The lower an individual's ability to lead, the lower the lid on his potential. So as the owner, your organization and its potential can only grow as far as you can take it. The level of your "lid" determines whether or not you will hit the Billion Dollar Bullseye.

Most people do not raise their levels high enough to achieve this outcome on their own.

How to Know You've Hit the People Target

You'll know you've hit the bullseye with People when you literally have them beating down your door to work at your company. If people hear from friends and family how amazing, enjoyable, wonderful, fulfilling, impactful, and rewarding the experiences working for you are, then you almost don't need to ever run an ad to source employees because you can simply ask for referrals.

People
Persuasion
Promotion
Prestige
Product
Profit
Purpose

Figure 10
The Expanded Bullseye: Purpose through People

Hitting the People target is the byproduct of having systems that are so masterfully designed that your employees feel like they are equipped for success. They get to bring their best selves to work because they're on a stage that they love performing on for an audience they enjoy performing for.

Nailing it with People means that you have designed the company to be as transformational and empowering for the people who work for it as it is for its customers. Your people are able to be at their best, do their best work, and be surrounded by others who are doing the same.

To truly hit the People target, all other targets on the Billion Dollar Bullseye must be nailed. In fact, if you have all the other rings of the Bullseye Formula locked in, you can't help but hit the People target.

Conclusion: Aiming for the Billion Dollar Bullseye

Let's come full circle.

In the introduction, I laid out the two reasons for writing this book.

1. To connect with the right people and businesses I can advise, partner with, or invest in to broaden our collective global impact.
2. To help you win as quickly as possible so that you're excited about the potential of #1.

I'll close the loop on #2 before bringing #1 home.

In our extensive journey through *Billion Dollar Bullseye*, I've laid out the seven core principles that form the bedrock of successful, scalable business growth: **Purpose, Profit, Product, Prestige, Promotion, Persuasion, and People.** As you can now appreciate, these principles aren't just lofty ideals but concrete strategies that entrepreneurs can leverage to achieve exceptional success in their ventures.

I'll say it again.

Entrepreneurs have a passion for the projects they find enjoyable, yet they frequently overlook the critical areas that truly contribute the most potential value to their businesses.

To attain growth in your business, you must reconsider your approach and shift your focus (p. 16).

Most importantly, your business is a wealth asset. If you're not growing it, you're derelict in your duty (p. 18).

So, with this in mind, let's recap each principle so that you finish this book with clarity, renewed purpose, and clear ideas on how to grow your business.

Purpose: The Heartbeat of a Business

Purpose is the foundational principle that sets the tone for your entire entrepreneurial journey. It's the driving force behind your business, answering the fundamental question of why it exists. Purpose is not a lofty idea when scaling and exiting your business. It's your bullseye. It's about building something worthwhile and sustainable.

Purpose Drives Solid Numbers

- A Gallup study found that organizations with highly engaged employees experience 23% higher profitability.[1]
- Companies with a strong commitment to customer experience have a 1.5 times higher employee engagement rate.[2]
- A Deloitte study found purpose-driven companies witness higher market share gains and grow on average three times faster than their competitors, all the while achieving higher employee and customer satisfaction.[3]

1   Sorenson, Susan. "The Benefits of Employee Engagement." *Gallup*, January 7, 2023. https://www.gallup.com/workplace/236927/employee-engagement-drives-growth.aspx.
2   RingCentral. "10 Stats That Show the Undeniable Connection between EX and CX." *RingCentral*, 2024. https://www.ringcentral.com/better-employee-engagement/10-stats-that-show-the-undeniable-connection-between-ex-and-cx/.
3   O'Brien, Diana, Suzanne Kounkel, Andy Main, and Anthony R. Stephan. "Purpose Is Everything." *Deloitte Insights*, October 15, 2019. https://www2.deloitte.com/us/en/insights/topics/marketing-and-sales-operations/global-marketing-trends/2020/purpose-driven-companies.html.

I encourage you to delve deeper into purpose-driven business and consider exploring the works of experts like Simon Sinek and Daniel Pink. Their books, such as *Start with Why* and *Drive*, offer more insights into the transformative power of purpose.

Implementing Purpose in Your Business

- **Define and articulate your internal purpose:** Know why you're undertaking this adventure, and make sure it's powerful enough to pull you through any obstacle.
- **Define and articulate your external purpose:** Clearly state why your business exists and what meaningful impact it aims to create for your customers. Make it intellectually, culturally, and physically obvious to everyone in your organization.
- **Align your team with your purpose:** Share your purpose openly with your team, partners, and customers to create a culture that values and supports it.
- **Continuously evaluate and refine your purpose:** Regularly assess if your actions and decisions align with your stated purpose and adjust as needed.

In this era of AI, genuine human connection will be your distinguishing factor. Publicly express your purpose, share your ongoing learning experiences, and prioritize authenticity. Foster a company culture where people rally behind your success because they understand your values, principles, and the community you serve (p. 186).

Profit: The Engine of Growth

Profit is not just about making money; it's about creating a sustainable model that fuels your business's growth and innovation. Profitability is the litmus test of your strategy's effectiveness.

A meticulously crafted pricing strategy is essential for achieving your dream exit. Pricing ranks among the foremost tools a business can employ to boost its valuation significantly (p. 67).

Profit Drives Opportunity

- A study by McKinsey & Company reveals that highly profitable companies are more likely to invest in research and development, ensuring they stay ahead of their competitors.[4]
- Profitable businesses are better positioned to attract top talent, as they can offer competitive compensation and growth opportunities.[5]
- Research from Accenture shows that 63% of companies reinvest their profits into the business to drive growth.[6]

To deepen your understanding of profitability and sustainable growth, consider exploring books like *Good to Great* by Jim Collins, *What the CEO Wants You to Know* by Ram Charan, and *Blue Ocean Strategy* by W. Chan Kim and Renée Mauborgne. These titles offer invaluable perspectives on the art of achieving both profitability and differentiation.

Implementing Profit in Your Business

- **Focus on sustainable profitability:** Strive to create a business model that generates consistent profits while reinvesting in growth and innovation.
- **Implement a well-planned pricing strategy:** Consider your pricing

---

4   Babcock, Ariel, Sarah Keohane Williamson, and Tim Koller. "How Executives Can Help Sustain Value Creation for the Long Term." *McKinsey & Company*, July 22, 2021. https://www.mckinsey.com/capabilities/strategy-and-corporate-finance/our-insights/how-executives-can-help-sustain-value-creation-for-the-long-term.
5   FasterCapital. "Attracting and Retaining Top Talent for Competitive Advantage." *FasterCapital*, March 2024. https://fastercapital.com/content/Attracting-and-Retaining-Top-Talent-for-Competitive-Advantage.html.
6   Accenture. *Driving Reinvention, Delivering 360° Value: Annual Report.* Accenture, 2023. https://www.accenture.com/content/dam/system-files/acom/custom-code/iconic/ir-360/pdf/Accenture-Fiscal-2023-Annual-Report.pdf.

strategy to maximize your valuation potential and ensure profitability.

- **Monitor key financial metrics:** Stay informed about your business's financial health by tracking key metrics like revenue, expenses, and profitability.

It is simple. No numbers, no business. Know numbers, know business (p. 49).

Product: The Epicenter of Success

Your product or service is your offering to the world, and its quality is paramount. A great product is the cornerstone of customer satisfaction, loyalty, and business success. It's essential to continuously refine and perfect your product, ensuring it addresses real problems and adds significant value to your customers.

Start big picture then work your way down.

1. What is your product promising your customer?
2. What job is your product being hired to do, and what other hires can be made to do that job? [7]

First and foremost, aim to capture that transformative customer experience. Afterward, supplement it with supporting details. Avoid getting overly absorbed in the specifics at the expense of your overarching promise.

Big Take Away: Do not, I repeat, do not rely on marketing to make your product stand out. It's a trap. Every time. And it will sink your profit margins. Make your product different enough to stand out on its own. How? Circle back to the top of the list. Research your market and listen to your customers (p. 87).

---

7   Ulwick, Tony. "Jobs-to-Be-Done: A Framework for Customer Needs." Medium, January 6, 2017. https://jobs-to-be-done.com/jobs-to-be-done-a-framework-for-customer-needs-c883cbf61c90.

Product Drives Loyalty

- According to a survey by Nielsen, 59% of consumers prefer to buy new products from brands familiar to them.[8]
- McKinsey reports that companies consistently delivering superior customer experience across their product offerings achieve 3X higher customer satisfaction and loyalty.[9]
- A recent study showed a company's aftersales service could improve the firm's long-term brand image and brand loyalty. The aftersales department has the potential to produce 80% of a company's profit and improve its operational performance indicators.[10]

For further insights into product development and delivering value, consider delving into books like *The Four Steps to the Epiphany* by Steve Blank, *Inspired* by Marty Cagan, and *The Innovator's Dilemma* by Clayton Christensen. These resources offer valuable guidance on crafting compelling products and fostering innovation.

Implementing Product in Your Business

- **Prioritize product excellence:** Continuously improve your product or service to meet customer needs and expectations.
- **Start with a clear value proposition:** Ensure your product addresses real problems and communicates its unique value to customers.
- **Embrace customer feedback:** Listen to and iterate on your product based on their input to enhance customer satisfaction.

8   Stokes, Jordan. "The Importance of Brand Recognition in the Consumer Purchase Decision." *GoRollick*, August 2018. https://gorollick.com/articles/press-release/the-importance-of-brand-recognition-in-the-consumer-purchase-decision/.

9   Briedis, Holly, Anne Kronschnabl, Alex Rodriguez, and Kelly Ungerman. "Adapting to the Next Normal in Retail: The Customer Experience Imperative." *McKinsey & Company*, May 14, 2020. https://www.mckinsey.com/industries/retail/our-insights/adapting-to-the-next-normal-in-retail-the-customer-experience-imperative.

10   Haryadi, Didit, Haerofiatna Haerofiatna, and Abdul Wahid Alfarizi. "The Role of After Sales Service on Customer Loyalty Mediated by Customer Satisfaction." *eCo-Buss* 5, No. 2 (December 2022): 583–592. https://www.researchgate.net/publication/366181346_The_Role_of_After_Sales_Service_on_Customer_Loyalty_Mediated_by_Customer_Satisfaction.

In the pursuit of business growth, maintaining flexibility is paramount. Stay open-minded and embrace experimentation to discover the strategies that resonate most effectively with your goals (p. 97).

Prestige: The Art of Building a Respected Brand

The notion of customer prestige serves as a powerful amplifier ring on our bullseye, as the compounding benefits derived from prioritizing this aspect of your business are truly immeasurable (p. 113).

People aren't going to remember anything except the way you made them feel. And this is another element of building that relationship with your customer (p. 115).

The authorities, including Al Ries and Jack Trout, Seth Godin, and Scott Bedbury, have shared their wisdom on crafting prestigious brands. Their works emphasize the need to stand out and create remarkable, aspirational brands.

Prestige Sets the Stage for Increased Value

- According to Nielsen, 66% of consumers are willing to pay more for products and services from companies that are committed to making a positive social and environmental impact.[11]
- According to Salesforce, 73% of customers are likely to switch brands if a company provides inconsistent levels of service.[12]

11   Forliance. "Why Investing in Sustainability Is a Smart Business Move." *Forliance*, March 7, 2023. https://forliance.com/news/2023/03/07/why-investing-in-sustainability-is-a-smart-business-move #:~:text=In%20fact%2C%20a%20study%20by%20Nielsen%20found%20that%2066%25%20of, also%20a%20smart%20business%20mov.
12   Salesforce Research. "Why Help Desk Software Reviews Are Serving Up a Better Customer Experience." *Salesforce*, 2024. https://www.salesforce.com/ap/hub/service/help-desk-software-reviews-matter/.

- HubSpot reports that 93% of customers are likely to make repeat purchases from companies that offer excellent customer service.[13]

To dive deeper into the world of brand building and reputation, consider exploring books like *A New Brand World* by Scott Bedbury, *Positioning: The Battle for Your Mind* by Al Ries and Jack Trout, and *Purple Cow* by Seth Godin. These texts provide valuable insights into building brand prestige and standing out in a crowded marketplace.

Implementing Prestige in Your Business

- **Build a prestigious brand:** Cultivate a reputation that sets your business apart and commands respect in the marketplace.
- **Focus on customer experience:** Prioritize providing exceptional customer service and support to enhance brand loyalty.
- **Exceed customer expectations:** Go above and beyond to surprise and delight customers, fostering positive word-of-mouth and trust.

So, it's simple. Listen.

Do you ask for feedback? Listen to it and act on it.

Then, add the magic and exceed expectations. Go above and beyond. Give your customers what they thought they needed and what they dreamed they wanted (p. 116).

When customers enjoy a positive experience with a brand, they tend to share that experience with others, ultimately resulting in heightened brand awareness and credibility—a phenomenon affectionately known as "word-of-mouth marketing" (p. 124).

---

13 Fontanella, Clint. 2024. "33 Customer Service Tips HubSpot Reps Swear By." HubSpot (blog). *HubSpot.* February 8, 2024. https://blog.hubspot.com/service/customer-service-tips#:~:text=According%20to%20HubSpot%20research%2C%2093,to%20get%20better%20customer%20service.

Promotion: Connecting with Your Audience

Promotion is not just about reaching people; it's about connecting with them, engaging them, and converting them into loyal customers. Promotion is the art of effectively communicating your value proposition to your target audience.

Experts like Eugene Schwartz, David Ogilvy, and Ann Handley have offered valuable insights into effective promotion and connecting with target audiences. Their work emphasizes the need for businesses to engage and convert customers through meaningful communication.

Promotion Promotes Profit

- A study by McKinsey & Co reveals that personalized promotional emails improve revenue by an average of 10-15%.[14]
- According to Statista, global social media ad spending reached $181 billion in 2021, highlighting the significance of digital promotion channels.[15]
- A survey by HubSpot found that 70% of marketers are actively investing in content marketing, recognizing its effectiveness in attracting and retaining customers.[16]

To refine your promotion strategies, consider exploring books like *Breakthrough Advertising* by Eugene Schwartz, *Ogilvy on Advertising* by David Ogilvy, *Talk Like TED* by Carmine Gallo, and *Everybody Writes* by Ann

14   Arora, Nidhi, Daniel Ensslen, Lars Fiedler, Wei Wei Liu, Kelsey Robinson, Eli Stein, and Gustavo Schüler. "The Value of Getting Personalization Right—or Wrong—Is Multiplying." *McKinsey & Company*, November 12, 2021. https://www.mckinsey.com/capabilities/growth-marketing-and-sales/our-insights/the-value-of-getting-personalization-right-or-wrong-is-multiplying.
15   Statista. "Social Media Advertising—Worldwide." *Statista*, n.d. https://www.statista.com/outlook/dmo/digital-advertising/social-media-advertising/worldwide.
16   Iskiev, Maxwell. *The 2024 State of Marketing & Trends Report: Data from 1400+ Global Marketers*. *HubSpot*, January 9, 2024. https://blog.hubspot.com/marketing/hubspot-blog-marketing-industry-trends-report.

Handley. These resources delve into the art of engaging communication and persuasive storytelling.

A big takeaway, especially when you start gathering intel and advice on this area, is one that I will die on the hill over. It is this.

Marketing is often an area where it's easy to stay busy without achieving meaningful results (p. 144).

So, be vigilant.

Implementing Promotion in Your Business

- **Create an effective communication strategy:** Develop a comprehensive plan to communicate your value proposition to your target audience.
- **Leverage digital channels:** Utilize digital marketing, social media, and content marketing to engage and convert customers.
- **Measure customer acquisition costs and lifetime value:** Analyze the costs of acquiring customers and focus on strategies that maximize their long-term value.

The key is to create a comprehensive strategy that combines these tactics in a way that is tailored to your target audience and supports your overall business goals (p. 138).

Persuasion: The Secret Sauce

Persuasion is the delicate art of convincing customers that your product or service is the solution they need. It's not about deception but about building trust, forging connections, and nurturing enduring relationships.

Hard selling is no longer effective; people seek conversations, solutions, partnerships, connections, and a sense of belonging. Even traditional car salesmen no longer rely on "selling"; it's all about fostering conversations (p. 156).

That's a fundamental truth. Treat people with respect. Acknowledge their intelligence and worth, for they are the very lifeblood of your business (p. 162).

Persuasion Influences People Behavior

Here are a few statistics that highlight the importance of persuasion:

- A survey by Edelman Trust Barometer reveals that 81% of consumers believe trust in a brand is a deal-breaker when deciding whether to buy from them.[17]
- **If you call a lead in the first 5 minutes after they've submitted a web form, they're 100x more likely to get on the phone.[18]**
- 85% of prospects and customers are dissatisfied with their on-the-phone experience.[19]

Esteemed authorities like Robert Cialdini, Dale Carnegie, and Daniel Pink have shared their insights into the psychology of persuasion and effective communication. Their work underscores the importance of authenticity, empathy, and building genuine relationships.

To deepen your understanding of persuasion, explore books like *Influence: The Psychology of Persuasion* by Robert Cialdini, *How to Win Friends and Influence People* by Dale Carnegie, and *To Sell Is Human* by Daniel Pink.

---

17   Edelman. "Only One-Third of Consumers Trust Most of the Brands They Buy." *Edelman*, June 18, 2019. https://www.edelman.com/news-awards/only-one-third-of-consumers-trust-most-of-the-brands-they-buy.
18   Verma, Anurag. "The Theory of Glengarry Glen Ross in the Era of IoT." Datamatics Business Solutions, 2024. https://www.datamaticsbpm.com/blog/the-theory-of-glengarry-glen-ross-in-the-era-of-iot/#:~:text=According%20to%20The%20Lead%20Response,intervention%20can%20help%20core%20salespeople.
19   Dang, Vy. "21 Sales Call Statistics to Raise Your Cold Calling Game." *Salestrail*, October 15, 2020. https://www.salestrail.io/blog/sales-call-statistics.

These texts offer valuable guidance on persuasion and building lasting customer relationships.

Implementing Persuasion in Your Business

- **Build trust and authenticity.** Establish trust with customers by being transparent, empathetic, and genuine.
- **Engage in meaningful conversations.** Shift from hard selling to building relationships and understanding customer needs.
- **Consistently provide value.** Focus on delivering ongoing value to customers to build long-lasting relationships and loyalty.

And always remember this golden rule: never lie or mislead. Ever (p. 161).

People: Consider Them Differently

Remember this.

Since humans can be unpredictable, it's wise not to place them at the core of your bullseye (p. 189).

Before you even contemplate the kind of individuals you want to bring into your company, ensure that all other aspects are meticulously in place. Keep in mind that the performance of your team is directly influenced by the environment you provide them with. It's unfair to talented individuals to onboard them into anything less than a well-organized and thriving business (p. 193).

To further explore the realm of organizational culture and leadership, consider reading books like *Delivering Happiness* by Tony Hsieh, *Drive* by Daniel Pink, and *Powerful* by Patty McCord. These resources offer valuable insights into creating workplaces that value people, innovation, and customer satisfaction, and get people to "buy in and stay in."

Implementing People in Your Business

- **Nurture a purpose-driven culture:** Create an environment where employees are motivated by the company's purpose.
- **Invest in talent development:** Support the growth and development of your team members to maximize their potential.
- **Put people at the center of your business:** Prioritize the well-being and satisfaction of your team, partners, and customers.

And above all, lead by example. You're doing something big here. You have the know-how and the vision. Your people might not have the whole picture. They're following you. Be worth following (p. 198).

Coming Full Circle

In wrapping up, *Billion Dollar Bullseye* is your trusty guide through the exhilarating world of entrepreneurship. Whether you're at the starting line or gearing up for your next big leap, these principles are your compass, navigating the way ahead.

Channeling the spirit of Zig Ziglar, our aim here isn't just to fuel your own dreams, but to empower you to uplift others along your journey. Sure, the road to entrepreneurial success is bumpy, but armed with the Bullseye Formula, you're equipped to tackle whatever comes your way.

Let's circle back to the heart of it all and the main reason I wrote this book. After retiring from Kajabi with all the success that brought, I finally felt able to help others have their own exit. By connecting with fellow trailblazers and businesses, I believe we can magnify our global impact. It's about rewriting the story of entrepreneurship—one where failure isn't the end but a stepping stone to greatness.

That's where the Bullseye Formula comes in. It's our secret weapon to defy the odds and carve out a path to success. My mission? To flip the script on entrepreneurial failure and help you write a story of resilience and triumph.

I believe that entrepreneurship is the single greatest transformational force in the world today, and it may just be the thing that saves it. Entrepreneurship changes lives, raises communities, and has the potential to impact the world. The world needs not just more entrepreneurs, but more successful entrepreneurs, committed to paying it forward. And if you've gotten this far, I'm glad you're here.

With the principles that make up the seven rings of the Billion Dollar Bullseye, it is possible to scale as big as you want, as fast as you want, and exit (if you want) on your terms. It's time to put them into action.

As we wrap up, remember: My team and I are here for you every step of the way. Reach out, and let's explore your business and how to take it to new heights.

Thanks for joining me on this journey. Here's to your victories and the ripple effect we'll create together.

It's YOUR time.

—JONATHAN "JCRON" CRONSTEDT

Suggested Reading List as You Continue to Evolve

Keep practicing! Here is a recommended reading list for the entrepreneur who recognizes greatness and knows that practice defines execution.

Simon Sinek

» **Book:** *Start with Why: How Great Leaders Inspire Everyone to Take Action*

» **Synopsis***: Simon Sinek emphasizes the importance of understanding and communicating the "why" or purpose behind a business to inspire and motivate employees and customers.*

John Mackey

» **Books***: Conscious Capitalism; The Whole Foods Diet*

» **Synopsis:** *John Mackey, co-founder and CEO of Whole Foods Market, explores conscious capitalism and the role of purpose in business, promoting a holistic approach to profit and social impact.*

Daniel Pink

» **Books***: Drive; To Sell Is Human*

» **Synopsis:** *Daniel Pink delves into the concept of purpose and motivation in the workplace, emphasizing the role of autonomy, mastery, and purpose in driving performance, as well as the art of persuasion in sales.*

Joan Magretta
- » **Book:** *Understanding Michael Porter: The Essential Guide to Competition and Strategy*
- » **Synopsis:** *Joan Magretta's work focuses on strategy and value creation, with this book exploring the concept of purpose in business strategy.*

Jim Collins
- » **Book:** *Good to Great: Why Some Companies Make the Leap... And Others Don't*
- » **Synopsis:** *Good to Great identifies companies that achieved exceptional long-term performance and provides insights into the factors that contributed to their success.*

Eric Ries
- » **Book:** *The Lean Startup: How Today's Entrepreneurs Use Continuous Innovation to Create Radically Successful Businesses*
- » **Synopsis:** *The Lean Startup focuses on lean thinking and continuous innovation to drive profitability and growth through testing and adapting business models.*

W. Chan Kim and Renée Mauborgne
- » **Book:** *Blue Ocean Strategy: How to Create Uncontested Market Space and Make the Competition Irrelevant*
- » **Synopsis:** *Blue Ocean Strategy introduces the idea of creating new market spaces (blue oceans) through innovation to achieve differentiation and profitability.*

Alexander Osterwalder and Yves Pigneur
- » **Book:** *Value Proposition Design: How to Create Products and Services Customers Want*
- » **Synopsis:** *This book provides a framework for creating customer-centric value propositions that drive profitability through understanding and addressing customer needs.*

Clayton Christensen

» **Book:** *The Innovator's Dilemma: When New Technologies Cause Great Firms to Fail*
» **Synopsis:** *The Innovator's Dilemma explores the challenges established companies face in maintaining profitability and competitiveness in the face of disruptive innovation, offering strategies for sustainable growth.*

Mike Michalowicz

» **Book:** *Profit First: Transform Your Business from a Cash-Eating Monster to a Money-Making Machine*
» **Synopsis:** *Profit First offers a unique perspective on managing profitability by prioritizing profit allocation from the outset, providing a practical framework for financial health.*

Philip Kotler, Kevin Lane Keller, and Alexander Chernev

» **Book:** *Marketing Management*
» **Synopsis:** *Philip Kotler's work emphasizes brand reputation and building customer loyalty through positive experiences, providing insights into marketing theory and practice.*

Seth Godin

» **Books:** *Purple Cow; Permission Marketing*
» **Synopsis:** *Seth Godin emphasizes creating remarkable, prestigious brands that stand out in the marketplace and capture consumers' attention.*

Scott Bedbury

» **Book:** *A New Brand World: Eight Principles for Achieving Brand Leadership in the Twenty-First Century*
» **Synopsis:** *Scott Bedbury offers insights into building and maintaining brand prestige and authenticity based on his experiences with iconic brands like Nike and Starbucks.*

Robert Cialdini

» **Book:** *Influence: The Psychology of Persuasion*
» **Synopsis:** *Robert Cialdini explores the psychology behind building credibility and prestige, discussing how businesses can leverage social proof and authority to enhance their reputation.*

Al Ries and Jack Trout

» **Book:** *Positioning: The Battle for Your Mind*
» **Synopsis:** *Al Ries and Jack Trout emphasize the importance of positioning a brand in consumers' minds to create a distinct and prestigious image.*

Daniel Kahneman

» **Book:** *Thinking, Fast and Slow*
» **Synopsis:** *Nobel laureate Daniel Kahneman's work provides insights into how consumer perceptions of prestige and credibility are formed and how businesses can influence them through decision-making.*

Guy Kawasaki

» **Book:** *Enchantment: The Art of Changing Hearts, Minds, and Actions*
» **Synopsis:** *Guy Kawasaki explores techniques for enchanting customers and creating a strong connection with them through persuasive communication.*

Richard Koch

» **Book:** *The 80/20 Principle: The Secrets to Achieving More with Less*
» **Synopsis:** *Be more effective with less effort by learning how to identify and leverage the 80/20 principle: that 80 percent of all our results in business and in life stem from a mere 20 percent of our efforts.*
» **Book:** *The Star Principle: How It Can Make You Rich*
» **Synopsis:** *Star businesses are ventures operating in a high-growth sector—and are the leaders in their niche of the market. Stars are rare. But with the help of this book and a little patience, you can find one, or create one yourself.*

Ann Handley

» **Book:** *Everybody Writes: Your Go-To Guide for Creating Ridiculously Good Content*

» **Synopsis:** Ann Handley emphasizes the importance of quality content in effective communication and promotion, urging businesses to become better storytellers to connect with their audience.

Ryan Holiday

» **Book:** *Trust Me, I'm Lying: Confessions of a Media Manipulator*

» **Synopsis:** Ryan Holiday discusses the modern media landscape and how businesses can manipulate it to gain attention, providing valuable insights into understanding media and communication.

Jay Baer

» **Book:** *Youtility: Why Smart Marketing Is about Help Not Hype*

» **Synopsis:** Jay Baer advocates being genuinely helpful to customers through content marketing and communication, emphasizing the importance of building trust through valuable, customer-focused communication.

Dale Carnegie

» **Book:** *How to Win Friends and Influence People*

» **Synopsis:** Dale Carnegie's classic work focuses on interpersonal communication and persuasion, emphasizing building genuine relationships and effectively persuading others.

Edgar Schein

» **Book:** *Organizational Culture and Leadership*

» **Synopsis:** Edgar Schein's book provides a framework for understanding and shaping corporate culture, emphasizing the role of leadership in this process.

Patrick Lencioni

» **Book:** *The Advantage: Why Organizational Health Trumps Everything Else in Business*

» **Synopsis:** *Patrick Lencioni discusses the importance of a cohesive leadership team and a healthy organizational culture in achieving success.*

Sylvia Ann Hewlett

» **Book:** *The Sponsor Effect: How to Be a Better Leader by Investing in Others*

» **Synopsis:** *Sylvia Ann Hewlett explores the role of sponsorship in nurturing talent and creating inclusive organizational cultures, focusing on talent and diversity in the workplace.*

Tony Hsieh

» **Book:** *Delivering Happiness: A Path to Profits, Passion, and Purpose*

» **Synopsis:** *In the late Tony Hsieh's book, he shares his experiences and insights on creating a workplace where people are passionate about the company's mission, emphasizing a customer-centric and employee-focused culture.*

Scott Adams

» **Book:** *Win Bigly: Persuasion in a World Where Facts Don't Matter*

» **Synopsis:** *Scott Adams discusses persuasion techniques in the context of politics and everyday life, exploring the art of persuasion.*

This comprehensive list covers various aspects of the Bullseye Formula, providing valuable personal and professional growth insights.

About the Author

Jonathan "Jcron" Cronstedt

Jonathan Cronstedt, widely known as JCron, epitomizes the essence of entrepreneurial brilliance and digital innovation. With a rich career spanning over
two decades, JCron has established himself as a vanguard in various sectors,
including SaaS, mortgage finance, digital publishing, and direct sales. He is
a luminary in digital innovation and entrepreneurial leadership.

JCron's educational backbone began at Concordia University Irvine, where
he earned a Bachelor of Arts in Business Administration. This foundational
education paved the way for his extraordinary career path, characterized by
strategic leadership and groundbreaking achievements.

Pioneering Growth and Strategy

JCron's prowess shone brightly during his tenure as President at Kajabi, a leading knowledge commerce platform. In five short years, Kajabi grew 2153%, catapulting Kajabi to a $2 billion valuation.

Before Kajabi, JCron held significant roles, including CEO of Digital Marketer and President of Prodigy Consulting Group. His tenure in these positions underscored his ability to foster growth and embrace technological advancements.

Currently, as a Board Director at Kajabi and Managing Partner at Apex Equity, JCron continues to impact the digital and investment landscapes profoundly.

JCron's influence extends beyond boardrooms into his personal and philanthropic realms. He and the family foundation are dedicated to empowering the next generation of entrepreneurs, reflecting his belief in entrepreneurship as a transformational global force.

Outside his professional sphere, JCron is a dedicated husband to Nicole, a loving father to Morgan Taylor, and a doting owner to his puppy, Stella. His passions include enjoying fine spirits and engrossing literature.

JCron is not just an accomplished business leader; he is a symbol of innovation, resilience, and human-centric leadership. His experiences and insights render him an invaluable speaker and mentor whose stories and strategies inspire and shape the contours of modern business and entrepreneurship.

Here's where you can find and follow the author: www.JCRON.com.

Glossary

A-player: Someone who excels at their job.

Accrual Accounting: A financial accounting method that recognizes income when the revenue is earned and records expenses when liabilities are incurred, regardless of when cash is received or paid.

Addressable Market: The total market demand for a product or service is usually calculated in annual revenue or unit sales.

Accounting Rate of Return (ARR): A formula that reflects the percentage rate of return expected on an investment or asset compared to the initial investment's cost.

BOGO: A sales promotion in which an item is offered free or at a reduced price when another item is purchased at full price.

Bootstrapped: A method of founding and running a company with little or no outside capital, relying on personal finances or operating revenue.

Bro-Marketing: Sales and marketing tactics that are manipulative and self-serving, designed to disempower clients and remove their agency, making them more susceptible to buying a service or product.

Burn Rate: The rate at which a company is losing money.

C-Level (C-Suite): The highest-ranking executives in a company or organization.

Capital Strategy: The company's plan or approach to manage its financial resources and investments, aiming to achieve long-term goals by maximizing returns and minimizing risk.

Cash Flow: The movement of money in and out of a company, measuring net cash and cash equivalents transferred in (inflows) and out (outflows).

Category Design: A business strategy and discipline that helps companies create, develop, and dominate new categories of products and service.

Crowdsource: The practice of obtaining needed services, ideas, or content by soliciting contributions from a large group of people, primarily online, rather than traditional employees or suppliers.

Customer Relationship Management (CRM): A set of integrated data-driven software solutions that manage, track, and store information about a company's current and potential customers.

Differentiators: The unique features or characteristics of a product, service, or company that set it apart from competitors and make it more attractive to customers.

Digital: In computing, anything based on electronics or computerized technology, including devices, data, or processes composed of binary digits (0 and 1).

Digital Download: A file or software that can be downloaded without requiring a physical product. They can be sold as digital products or provided for free by creators (often in exchange for the user's email address).

Double Unicorn: A company that has achieved a valuation of over $2 billion.

Dumb Money: Investors who make investment decisions based on instinct or gut feeling rather than careful market analysis or investment fundamentals.

EDLP (Everyday Low Prices): A pricing strategy that sets a low price and maintains it over a long period as long as the product costs remain unchanged.

Employee Burden Rate: The indirect costs associated with employees, such as payroll taxes, workers' compensation,

paid time off, training, travel expenses, pension contributions, and other benefits, in addition to gross compensation.

Fixed Costs: Expenses that remain constant regardless of production or sales levels, not directly related to producing goods or services. Also considered indirect costs.

Great Resignation: A recent trend of employees leaving their jobs in record numbers after the COVID-19 pandemic, often attributed to factors like burnout, dissatisfaction with work-life balance, and a desire for more flexibility and autonomy.

Gross Profit Margin: A financial metric that measures a company's profitability by calculating the percentage of revenue remaining after deducting the cost of goods sold.

Growth Spend: The money spent to ensure that a company's growth is sustainable.

Hosting Package: A bundle of services offered by a web hosting company to its customers, typically including web hosting, email hosting, domain registration, etc.

In Cash Accounting: Recording revenues and expenses when cash is received and paid, respectively.

Institutional Capital: Invested in a financial institution by its members or other institutions to finance productive assets such as loans.

Key Performance Indicator (KPI): A quantifiable measurement to gauge a company's long-term performance.

Marketing Funnel: A model illustrating the customer journey from awareness to purchase, typically including stages like awareness, consideration, conversion, and loyalty.

Metrics: Quantitative assessment measures commonly used for evaluating, comparing, and tracking performance or production.

Net Profit Margin: A financial metric measuring how much net income or profit a company generates as a percentage of its revenue.

Net Revenue Retention (NRR): A metric used to measure the growth or decline of revenue streams tied to existing customers within a given time period.

Network Effect: A phenomenon in which the value of a product or service increases as more people use it.

Omnichannel: A business strategy to provide a seamless and high-quality customer experience within and between contact channels.

Online Platform: Digital services that facilitate interactions between distinct but interdependent sets of users, whether firms or individuals, who interact through the service via the internet.

OpEx (Operating Expenses): Expenses incurred by a company in its day-to-day operations, such as rent.

Optimizing: In computer science, the process of rewriting instructions in a program to maximize efficiency and speed in retrieval, storage, or execution.

Order of Operations: A set of rules dictating the order in which mathematical operations should be performed.

Outside Capital: Funds raised from investors not part of the company, used to accelerate growth, provide shareholder liquidity, or invest in new locations.

Perspective Sales Process: A consultative approach to selling that involves providing buyers with new knowledge to help them see their problem differently to achieve their business goals.

Performance Improvement Plan (PIP): A formal document outlining an employee's challenges, goals, and timelines for improvement.

Profit: The financial gain realized when the revenue generated from an activity exceeds the expenses, costs, and taxes involved in sustaining the activity.

Quiet Quitting: Doing the minimum requirements of one's job and putting in no more time, effort, or enthusiasm than necessary.

Research and Development (R&D): The process of innovation and experimentation companies undertake to create new products and services or improve existing ones.

Return on Investment (ROI): A financial metric used to evaluate the profitability of an investment or compare the efficiency of different investments.

Revenue: The total amount of money generated from normal business operations.

Software as a Service (SaaS): A software licensing and delivery model in which software is licensed on a subscription basis and is centrally hosted.

Sales Funnel: A marketing concept describing a potential customer's journey from awareness to purchase.

Scalable Business: A business capable of growing without being limited by available resources, where increased revenues cost less to deliver than current revenues.

Scale: Increasing revenue faster than costs enables a company to grow and expand its operations.

Social Proof: In marketing, leveraging positive feedback, endorsements, and testimonials from satisfied customers to influence potential buyers.

Split Test: A marketing strategy that compares two or more versions of an asset (e.g., a web page or email) to determine which version performs better in achieving a specific outcome, such as a higher click-through rate or conversion rate.

Stick Rate: Customer stickiness refers to the likelihood of a customer purchasing from a brand.

Index